HER OWN WAY
The Story of Lottie Moon

Her Own Way

THE STORY OF LOTTIE MOON

Helen A. Monsell

Illustrated by HENRY C. PITZ

BROADMAN PRESS
Nashville, Tennessee

© 1958 • Broadman Press
Nashville, Tennessee

Fifth Printing
424-044

Library of Congress Catalog Card Number 58-9919
Printed in the United States of America
3.5JE6513

CONTENTS

CONTENTS

HER OWN WAY
The Story of Lottie Moon

1
Apples Are Ripe

IT WAS a summer morning at Viewmont, the Moon's plantation-farm in the foothills of Virginia. The year was 1850.

Lottie sat on the porch steps of the Big House with her lap full of green cornshucks. She was making a cornshuck doll baby.

"We'll play you are ten years old," she told the doll. "That is how old I am. It is the very best age to be."

The cornshuck doll baby bobbed her head.

"You are old enough then to do all sorts of

things. And you are young enough to do them, too."

The doll's head wobbled as if it were trying to say "That doesn't make good sense."

"But it *does* make good sense," Lottie insisted. "Take climbing trees, for instance. My little sisters are too young. Mary would fall before she reached the first branch. So would Sarah. My big sister Orie, though, is too old. Why, she is almost a young lady! Young ladies must never climb trees. But ten-years-old is just right."

Lottie pulled the cornshucks into shape.

"There! Let's see how you look." She held the new doll baby up and turned her around carefully. "Your sash isn't tight enough. I can hardly tell your waist from your skirts. Hold still now while I pull it tighter."

She gave a quick tug to the blade of ribbon grass that was tied around the middle of the cornshucks. Then——

"Oh, my goodness!"

The grass had broken. The cornshucks fell apart.

"That is just the trouble with you cornshuck dolls," Lottie scolded. "You never last long enough to pay me for making you."

She threw her cornshucks away and jumped up.

"I am tired of playing dolls anyway. Come along, Shep, let's go for a run over the hills."

A big dog had been lying by the hammock in the yard. He jumped up quickly. It was plain that he thought a run over the hills would be a good idea. Girl and dog raced off together.

At the yard gate she stopped short. A thicket of honeysuckle grew over the fence there. The air was heavy with its sweet odor. Lottie picked a blossom and bit off the end. Then she drew out the long pistil. There was a drop of nectar at its tip. Tiny as it was, it had a wonderful taste.

"Um-m! Wouldn't a whole spoonful be grand?" Lottie asked the dog.

She raced back to the kitchen to ask old Aunt Sukey for a spoon. Lottie never walked when she could run. Then she gathered a big armful of honeysuckle sprays and dropped down on the grass.

Shep looked disgusted. This was no way to go for a run. He lay down in the shade of the honeysuckle thicket. Maybe Lottie wouldn't play very long at this new game either.

She didn't. The nectar drops were so tiny it would take ages just to wet the bottom of the spoon. Lottie wasn't going to sit still that long.

"All right, Shep. Let's really go this time." She jumped up again. The honeysuckle fell to the ground as the cornshucks had done.

"If we stop to unfasten the gate, we'll have to fasten it up again. It will be easier if you just crawl under," she told Shep. "I'll climb over. And I'll just leave my spoon on the gate post until we get back."

She was so busy climbing that she didn't see the boy on horseback who was riding up the lane from the road. The horse was big, but the boy wasn't much taller than Lottie. There was a row of

"I'll climb over," she told Shep.

freckles on his nose. He was whistling a cheerful tune. He had almost reached the gate before she knew he was there.

"Hello!" he said suddenly.

Lottie was so startled that she nearly fell off the gate. "Goodness me, Jim Moon! You just about scared me out of my skin."

Her cousin grinned. "Whatever you are doing, you always do it mighty hard, don't you?"

Lottie grinned, too. "It's faster that way. And I like to do things *quick!*"

"How about a quick run back down to the road with me? The apples on that tree in the old field are getting ripe. I tried one as I came along."

Lottie forgot about the run over the hills. "Let's go right away. But I'll get us a basket first. Then we can bring some back to Mother and the others."

"I don't know whether we can find enough ripe ones to fill a basket."

"Then we'll bring back some of the little green ones, too. I'll make some green apple doll babies after dinner. They won't fall apart the way corn-shuck babies do."

"All right."

"I'll go get the basket and tell Mother that you are here. You're going to stay to dinner, aren't you?"

"Well, Mother sent me over with a note for Aunt Anne, but she didn't say anything about hurrying home."

"Then of course you'll stay. Give me the note to take Mother while you ride on down to the stable. I'll meet you here at the gate. Now don't you get so interested in that new colt in the stable that you keep me waiting."

"I'll be back before you are," Jim promised.

He was right. Lottie was breathless with hurrying when she reached the yard gate again, but Jim was already there. He was sitting on the gatepost as if he had been there all the morning.

"Slow poke!" he teased.

"I couldn't help it. Mammy made me wait for

"I'll race you to the road."

my sunbonnet. She tied it on so tight it will never come off. I don't see why folks fuss if a little girl's cheeks get a bit tanned. If it is all right for boys to have freckles, why can't girls have them, too? It is *hot* under this bonnet!"

"Is it too hot to run? I'll race you to the road."

"All right. Are you ready? One—two—three—Go!"

The two cousins were off. Shep raced along with

them. Dust rose in puffs beneath their feet. Lottie's two long braids bobbed up and down on her back. This time it was she who won.

"You can certainly run," Jim told her.

Across the road was an open field. It was fringed with weeds and blackberry bushes. An old apple tree grew there, close by the road. Its branches were so low Lottie felt that it was almost begging to be climbed. Getting up, though, wasn't as easy as it looked.

Jim climbed up first. Then he reached down for the basket. Lottie stood on tiptoe to hand it up to him. He hung it on a small branch. Then he leaned down again and gave Lottie his hand so that he could help her up to the first branch.

"I could climb up ever so much better," Lottie told him, "if it weren't for my skirts. They keep getting in the way. I wish I could wear boys' clothes when I play outdoors."

"You would look a sight! Imagine a girl wearing trousers!"

"Chinese girls do. I've seen a picture of them."

She climbed out on a long limb and held on carefully with one hand while she reached up with the other to pull down a red apple.

"But I don't believe it would be very easy for them to climb trees, even then," Jim told her. "What with their poor little feet bound so tight and hurting so terribly."

"You are right." Lottie was so interested in the Chinese children she stopped her apple picking. "Do you know, when I was a little girl I tried to dig my way through the ground to China once?"

"How far did you get?"

"Oh, I dug and dug, until Mammy called me to come take my nap. And when I waked up—"

"Lottie! Lottie!" A little girl in a pinafore was coming down the lane. She was calling anxiously. "Lottie!"

"Sh'h!" said Lottie. "There is Sarah. If she sees us, she'll want to climb up, too. And she is too little."

"Lottie!" Sarah was nearer now. "Where are you? Mother is ready to read to us."

"Oh!" Lottie began to climb down so quickly she almost fell head first.

"Hold on!" Jim reached down and caught her. "What is the rush? That could have been a bad tumble. And you haven't half filled the basket yet."

"The apples can wait. Didn't you hear what Sarah said? Mother is ready to read to us."

"What if she is? Is that any reason for you to start off like a puppy dog after a rabbit? She isn't in any such rush as all that."

"Maybe she isn't, but I am. If we don't get there right away someone will call her to do something else. They will want her down at the spring house, or one of the servants will get hurt and have to be bandaged up, or Father will ask her to help him find something."

"I know," said Jim. "It is just that way with my mother, too."

"Once she has actually started to read, though, we are safe. It would be impolite then for anyone to interrupt. That is why I am hurrying."

"All right. I'll hurry, too. Let me jump down first. Then I can reach up and steady you. There!"

They were on the ground again.

"You left your basket," said little Sarah.

"Shucks, I'll have to climb back up."

Jim turned toward the tree again but Lottie stopped him. "Let it stay where it is. We can get it after dinner. Right now, I tell you, we've got to hurry."

And hurry they did.

2
Books and Berries

THEY raced back up the lane to the house almost as quickly as they had raced down, but it was of no use. The front door of the big hall was wide open to catch the breeze. Mother's chair was there. Her little brown book was on the stand close by. But Mother was gone.

Orie was sitting on the hall sofa with her embroidery. "Sukey is making preserves and needed more sugar. Mother had to go to the storeroom," she told Lottie.

"What did I tell you?" Lottie asked Jim. She

dropped down into an old rocking chair and tugged at her bonnet strings.

Jim wiped the perspiration from his face. Shep flopped down near the door, panting.

"She said she would be right back, though," Orie added. "And she wanted you to start stitching the hems on the sleeves in Father's shirt."

"Maybe I had better go wash up a little first." Lottie looked at her hands.

"I should say so! How did you manage to get them so potty-black?"

"Cornshucks and tree bark and apple juice—but it will all wash off."

Lottie hurried back to Mother's room. There Mammy poured some water into the bowl for her from the big pitcher on the wash stand. When Lottie went back to the hall her hands were as clean as cold water and good soft soap could make them.

She got the rolls of soft white linen from her mother's work basket. Two kittens had taken her place in the old rocking chair. She tilted them gently to the floor. Jim found a piece of string in his pocket. He drew it along the floor in front of the kittens, and they pounced on it with delight. Lottie laughed as she watched them, but she kept a careful eye on the back door.

"I wish Mother would hurry up. The dinner bell will ring before she has had time to read a single page."

"Usually you can hardly wait for the dinner bell to ring," Jim told her. "What *is* this book that you are so anxious about? It must be a dandy!"

Jim found a piece of string in his pocket.

"It is. And it is every word true, too. It is all about Mrs. Ann Judson. She was a missionary to Burmah, you know. And we have just reached the place where the heathen soldiers have put her husband into prison, and she is afraid they are going to chop his head off. She has gone to the governor to try to save him, but the governor says 'You can do nothing more for your husband. Take care of yourself.' Then she—"

"Has Mother got back yet?" Sarah came trudging up the steps. She was almost big enough to start sewing but not quite.

"She can still do as she pleases, while I have to stitch for hours," Lottie thought. "It isn't fair. But then, I don't have to go to bed nearly as early as she does. Maybe that evens things up."

"I ran down to the mulberry tree while we were waiting," the little girl told them.

"Anyone could guess that," Orie laughed.

She was certainly right. Sarah's mouth was smeared with mulberry juice. There was a big stain on her apron. There were even purple spots on her hair.

"Why didn't you bring us some of the berries?" Jim teased.

"I couldn't. They are too squshy," she answered seriously.

"I never go near that mulberry tree if I can help it," Orie said. "It has almost as many worms on it as there are berries."

Sarah bobbed her head up and down. "Lots and lots of worms," she agreed. "Are they worms that make silk?"

"No. We've never kept silkworms here at Viewmont. Uncle James used to, though, years ago, when he still owned Monticello. He had quite a few mulberry trees there. I reckon he gave Mother ours."

"It was before we were born," Jim told her, "but I have heard Father tell about it. All over the country people went wild about growing mulberry trees. Every farm was going to raise silkworms.

The farmers' wives and children were going to unwind the cocoons and spin the thread. Even the poorest woman would have a silk dress to wear to church on Sunday."

"That would have been nice," Lottie said. "Why didn't it work out that way?"

"Oh, lots of reasons. American children didn't have the skill that Chinese children did when it came to unwinding the tiny threads. I reckon they didn't have the patience either."

"And they probably had too much else to do," Lottie told him severely.

"Maybe so. Besides, a blight struck the trees. And, all of a sudden, everyone grew tired of the whole thing. So now, most folks just keep mulberry trees in their yards because they are pretty."

"But they still have plenty of worms to eat their leaves even if they aren't silkworms."

"Um-*hum!*" little Sarah agreed. "I *hate* worms!"

A mischievous look came into Lottie's eyes. She reached over quietly and picked up a loose bit of worsted from Orie's work basket. She hid her hands beneath the rolls of linen in her lap, so that Sarah couldn't see what she was doing. She turned and twisted the worsted until it was just the size of a soft, squshy worm.

"Come here," she called to Sarah. "I believe I see a worm crawling on your shoulder now."

"Ugh!" Sarah came running over. "Get him off!"

"Turn around," Lottie commanded. Then she dropped the bit of worsted down the little girl's back. "No, there is nothing here. Maybe it crawled down the neck of your dress."

"Ow!" Sarah twisted and squirmed. She reached her arm around and tried to run her hand down her back. Just beyond her reach her finger tips could feel the soft, scratchy worsted.

"It is squirming!" she cried. "Get it out, Lottie! Quick! *Quick!*"

"Say please!" Lottie commanded.

"Please! Pretty please!"

Lottie thrust her hand down the back of the little girl's dress and drew out the worsted. "Why, it's only a piece of worsted from Orie's basket!" she exclaimed. Her voice was very innocent. "You were the one who was doing the squirming. But how in the world did it get way down your back like that? Poor little sister! Afraid of a piece of worsted!"

"Lottie!" said big sister Orie.

Sarah looked at her sister suspiciously. Had that worsted got down her back by itself, or was Lottie up to one of her tricks?

Then before she could make up her mind, Mother came through the back door. "I am sorry I was delayed," she said, "but we still have a few minutes before dinner."

The Moon children never quarreled in front of Mother. Besides, there was no time for it now. Sarah dropped the worsted worm to the floor. The kittens pounced on it with delight, while she ran to get Mother a fan. Jim pulled the big chair close to the door. Lottie hurried to get the little brown book.

"Here it is, Mother. You left off on page 303. We have just reached the place where the heathen soldiers have put her husband into prison and she is afraid they are going to chop his head off. 'With a heavy heart I went to my room—'"

"You left off on page 303."

Mother took the book and began to read. As Lottie listened, her comfortable Virginia home seemed to fade away. Instead she saw Mrs. Judson in her jolting cart. The Burmah sun was blazing down. She could smell the hot dust. She—

"Dong! Dong!" went the dinner bell.

Mother closed the book. "Fold up your work neatly, Lottie. Then go let Mammy tidy you and Sarah for dinner. Tell her to put a clean pinafore on Sarah."

It was hard for Lottie to come back to Viewmont. Her eyes had a faraway look as she went to Mother's room with Sarah. It was still there when she took her place at the dinner table.

"Here!" her brother Thomas teased. "Come back from wherever you are."

"I know how to fetch her home," said her brother Isaac. "Father, ask her which piece of chicken she wants."

"The neck, maybe?" Father asked with a twinkle in his eye.

Isaac was right. Lottie came back to Viewmont in a hurry. "You *know* I always want a drumstick."

Everybody laughed. Lottie's face clouded. She didn't like to be teased. Then she remembered that Orie had taught her how to stop them. She laughed, too.

Father gave her a quick smile. Lottie knew he was glad she hadn't turned sulky. He put an extra spoonful of gravy on her potatoes.

There was corn on the cob for dinner, too. It was the first time they had had corn that summer. And there was a dish of the new preserves to eat on their hot biscuits. No wonder Mrs. Judson faded into the back of Lottie's mind. But she didn't disappear entirely. She stayed—and stayed—and stayed.

3
Cookies and Company

I T SEEMED as if in no time at all the summer was almost over. Blackberries and raspberries were gone. Father had swung a hammock between the two horse chestnut trees down in the yard. As Lottie sat there she could see red leaves on the dogwood tree back of the house.

The hammock wasn't exactly comfortable. It was made of barrel slats and rope. If she didn't balance herself exactly in the middle it dumped her out. But it would soon be put away for the winter. She had better use it while she could. She put her foot down to push; then drew it back quickly before she upset.

She had had a busy morning. She had practiced her scales for an hour. She had studied her French verbs. She had covered a whole side of her slate with sums. Now surely she had earned an hour to do as she pleased. Only what did she please? Should she make come acorn teacups for Sarah's dolls? Her own dolls had plenty. Should she go for a run with the dogs?

Just then one of the dogs came up to find out why she was keeping so still. He poked his wet nose through the barrel slats. Lottie put her hand down to pet him, and the hammock spilled her to the ground. The dog jumped at her with delighted little barks. Lottie rolled over, laughing. She pretended to grab at him. They were right in the middle of a grand romp when Mammy came across the lawn.

"Miss Lottie! Wherever is you at, child? Your Ma is waiting for you."

Lottie pushed the dog away and sat up. She threw her braids back over her shoulder and tried to smooth the hair above her forehead.

The dog didn't want to stop. He begged her with little yelps to keep on playing.

"I'd like to," she told him, "but Mother probably wants me to practice some more. Or maybe my stitches were too big on those ruffles I was hemming. Goodness! I hope I don't have to do them all over again!"

Whatever it was Mother wanted, Lottie knew she mustn't keep her waiting. No sir! Mother was small. She almost never raised her voice, but when she said "Come," her children came.

She stood at the back door as Lottie crossed the yard. She had a small basket in her hand. It was full of big keys. Lottie knew them well. One was for the storeroom. One was for the meat house. One was for the cupboard where the preserves were kept. And there were goodness knew how many more!

"We're going out to the kitchen," said Mother. "It is high time for you to learn something about cooking."

Cooking! That was the last thing Lottie wanted to do. She pouted. "Why? When I grow up I'll always have servants to cook for me."

"Who will teach them how?"

"You'll let me have someone you have already taught."

"And how will you know whether she is doing things the right way or not?"

Lottie couldn't think of a good answer to that.

"Every girl," Mother went on, "should learn to cook and sew. She should learn how to take care of the sick. Maybe she will never have to do it. But then again, maybe she will."

"Mother certainly likes to preach!" thought Lottie to herself, but she didn't say it out loud.

The kitchen was in a little house by itself. It had its own big chimney and fireplace. It had its own kitchen yard.

One or two little Negro children were usually playing in the yard. They ran errands for old Aunt Sukey, the cook. They carried the covered dishes from the kitchen over to the dining room in the Big House. They helped shell peas and husk corn and beat the dough for beaten biscuit. They didn't get inside the kitchen very often, though. Aunt Sukey didn't like to have children under foot in her kitchen.

She wouldn't even let Lottie come in very often. She would fuss and fume and shoo her out as if she were a troublesome chicken. But when Mother, herself, brought Lottie in, Aunt Sukey didn't scold. She thought everything Mother did was all right. So did every other man, woman, and child on the plantation. Now she cleared the big kitchen table for them to use.

"Do you want me to build up the fire around the oven?"

Mother nodded. "Yes. I shall teach Lottie how to make cookies today."

Lottie had been looking through the open door. Her dog had left the yard now. He was chasing across the big field toward the Ragged Mountains. What fun it would be to race with him instead of working in this hot kitchen! But when Mother said "cookies" her face brightened. Cookies would be fun, too.

"May I have them all myself after I've made them?" she asked.

Mother looked troubled. "Wouldn't it be rather selfish to eat them all yourself?"

"Oh, goodness! I don't want to *eat* them! I want to take a plateful to Father and give Sarah some for a doll tea party. I'll save some for Jim and—"

Mother laughed. "You had better wait until you see how they turn out. Now, let's go to the storeroom for the flour and sugar."

Aunt Sukey had already sent one of the children in the yard for an armload of wood to build up the fire. Mother called to her to come help carry the heavy bowls. She let Lottie pick out the storeroom key from the key basket and turn it in the big, clumsy lock.

Back again in the kitchen, she showed her how to cream the butter and sugar together with a big wooden spoon.

"Now break your eggs carefully. Measure your milk in this cup. Next, you add the flour, a very little at a time. Stir it until it is smooth."

Lottie had never realized that making cookies was so much work.

"This is a very special way to make cookies," said Mother. "Your great-grandmother taught it to my mother. She taught it to me. Now I am teaching it to you."

Mother looked into Lottie's bowl.

"There!" she said. "I believe your dough is stiff enough. Put flour on your board and on your rolling pin. Now pinch off a piece of the dough and roll it very, very thin. Then you can use this glass tumbler to cut the cookies."

"You forgot the flour."

Lottie held the rolling pin tight. It wouldn't roll the way she wanted it to. The dough stuck to it.

"You forgot the flour," said Mother.

The first cookies were thick and ragged.

"Try again."

Lottie tried again. She rolled her dough so hard that her forehead was covered with beads of perspiration. Finally her hands began to understand what she wanted them to do. The next panful was better. In the next, the cookies came from the oven crisp and paper thin. Their spicy odor filled the kitchen.

"These are the ones I'll give Father," Lottie decided.

She was just putting the last batch into the oven when Sarah came running to the kitchen door.

"Company's coming! A carriage just turned into the lane!"

There was nothing unusual about having company. Hardly a week went by that some friend or cousin didn't come at least to spend the day. But company while Lottie was in the middle of baking cookies!

"Hurry!" said Mother. She was already taking off her apron. Aunt Sukey was pouring water into a basin for them to wash their hands. They almost ran back to the Big House. But they were standing at the front door to welcome their guests when they drove up.

Sarah was the first one out of the carriage. After she had called Mother she had run down the lane to meet the company and ride back with them. Then came Uncle James Barclay. He turned to help Aunt Julia and their daughter Sarah out.

Lottie always felt shy when Uncle James and his family came to visit them. It wasn't just because Uncle James had once owned President Thomas Jefferson's home at Monticello. It wasn't because Cousin Sarah was so young-ladyfied. It was because all of them were so very good.

Just look at Aunt Julia's hands, for instance. There wasn't a single ring on them. And Lottie knew why. She had given them all to help send a missionary to the heathen. You couldn't help feeling shy with anyone as good as that!

And now Uncle James was going to be a missionary himself. He was going to take his whole family with him.

"We'll be leaving next week," he was telling Mother. "There are many things we must finish before we go. Of course we are in a rush. We can't do more than spend the night with you, but we had to come to tell you good-by."

"Of course you had to," Mother agreed. "Lottie, will you go find your father? He won't want to miss a single minute of this visit."

Lottie started out to find Father. There were so many places he could be. Was he at the stables? Or the barns? Or down where the men were working in the river lot? He had said something this morning about riding over to see about cutting down some trees in the woodland across the river. Goodness! If he had gone that far it would take ages to send someone after him. But she caught him just before he left.

It wasn't until they were passing the kitchen on their way back to the house that she remembered her cookies. They would be burned to a crisp!

They weren't. Aunt Sukey had taken them from the oven, and they were cooling on the table. Yum-m-m! They smelled good. Lottie could tell that old Aunt Sukey was almost as proud of them as she was, but she wouldn't say so. Aunt Sukey believed that to praise a child to her face would make her conceited. Now she pretended to grumble just as she always did.

"How am I ever going to start fixing dinner with these here cookies all over the table?" she fussed.

C656594

"The first ones are cool enough to pack in the stone crock now," Lottie told her. She sounded almost as grown-up as Mother. "We'll put the warm ones on a plate. And you can send one of the children down to the spring house for a pitcher of cool milk."

Back in the parlor, the grownups were settling down for a long talk. Uncle James was telling Mother and Father about his plans. Thomas and Orie, in the corner by the sofa, were listening to Cousin Sarah.

"We are going to Jerusalem," she was saying. "Won't that be exciting? We'll see the hills where

David watched his sheep. We'll walk the same paths that Jesus walked. I am taking plenty of pencils and paper so that I can draw pictures of it all."

Just then she looked up. "Why, there is Lottie!"

And there was Lottie at the door. The house boy was with her. He was carrying a heavy tray. There were tall glasses on the tray, with a pitcher of milk. And there was a plate of crisp, warm cookies.

Lottie made them a curtsey. "I thought you might like a little refreshment before dinner," she said.

It sounded very dignified and important. She was downright proud of herself. But Thomas grinned.

"She means she has brought us a snack."

Lottie's face grew red.

Then Thomas bit into a cookie. He grinned again and this time it was a nice grin.

"My little sister can make good cookies," he told

his cousin. "You won't find any better ones in all Jerusalem."

Cookies in Jerusalem! Lottie laughed. Thomas had given her an idea, though. She thought about it as she began to sip her own glass of milk.

"It doesn't make any difference what country children live in, they like good things to eat." Her thoughts turned from Jerusalem to Mrs. Judson in Burmah. Then she thought of the poor little girls in China with their bound feet. She imagined them eating her cookies.

"And they would like them, too!"

4

No Time to Be Afraid

Turn around, honey," said Mammy, "and let me see if you are buttoned up right in the back. There! You look pretty as a posy. Just you go sit in the hall like a little lady, now, until your Ma and Pa are ready."

Lottie didn't like to sit in the hall like a little lady. Even pretending she was a grown lady come to pay a call didn't help. She was glad when Sarah joined her. Sarah wore her Sunday frock, too. Her lace-trimmed pantalets peeped out beneath her full skirts.

"It doesn't seem right to dress up in our Sunday clothes on Saturday," she told Lottie.

Lottie nodded. "Going to church on Saturday and Sunday both is like having two Sundays in a row. Only on Saturday we can play games after church is over."

Sarah leaned down to make sure her slipper ribbons hadn't come untied. "Do you know what?" she asked. "Cousin Mary says that in the big city churches they don't ever have Saturday preaching."

"They don't need to. They have it every Sunday. But our preacher lives so far away he can't get to us more than twice a month. So when he does come he preaches on Saturdays and Sundays both."

"Oh!" Sarah thought about it a moment. "Well, I like our way best, even if we do have to get all dressed up on Saturday. Because then we can spend the night in between at Cousin Mary's."

Lottie agreed. "Remember the fun we had last

time? There were so many children we had to sleep on pallets on the floor. And I rolled off during the night, and—"

Just then Father and Mother came to the door. "Are you ready, girls? It is a long drive to Scottsville."

Lottie felt, sometimes, as if the church at Scottsville just about belonged to the Moons. Mother had helped start it. Father had helped build it. There were ever so many Moon cousins in the pews. She knew that it would never do for a Moon daughter to go to sleep in church, and she honestly tried to listen to the sermon. She wondered, though, how much older she must be before she could really enjoy it the way Mother did.

After church the grown folks stood around to visit with each other a little, but Lottie and Sarah ran on ahead to Cousin Mary's. Cousin Mary's house had a big yard. Its bushes and hedges looked as if they had been planted especially to give children good places to play "Hiding." Lottie could hardly wait until supper was over so that they could begin.

It would have been a long wait even if she hadn't been in such a hurry. The grownups had their supper first. The children must wait for the second table.

"Let's tell ghost stories," someone suggested. "You first, Jim. Make it good and scary."

Jim sat down on the top porch step. The other children gathered around him.

"Once there was an old man," he began.

No one noticed when Lottie slipped away.

There was a pile of sheets in the upstairs hall. They would be used to make up the pallet beds. She borrowed one very quietly. Then she slipped down the back stairs and out into the yard through the side door. There was a big snowball bush by the porch. She crept behind it to wrap herself in the sheet.

Jim's ghost story was "good and scary" all right. The children were huddled close to him.

"It was the hour of midnight," Jim was saying. "Something white flapped in the bushes. There came a groan—"

"Ooo-oo-oo!" wailed Lottie behind the snowball bush. She almost scared herself.

The children jumped! What was that?

"Oooh! Oooh!" she went again. "Oooh-oo-oo!"

Lottie picked up a stick and draped the sheet around that, too. Now she poked it out beyond

"Ooo-oo-oo!" wailed Lottie.

the bush. It looked like a long, white arm. Slowly she moved out, herself. She came toward the porch. The sheet waved and flapped around her.

"Oooh! Oooh!" she wailed.

One of the children screamed. They all fell in a heap, huddling together.

She pointed her stick at Jim. "James Moon, beware!"

They fell in a heap, huddling together.

Her voice sounded as spooky as her groan, but Jim only laughed.

"You quit your nonsense, Lottie Moon! Scaring us poor children like that!"

It was kind of Jim to pretend he had been scared, too. It made the other children feel better. They began to giggle. "We knew you all the time."

Lottie dropped her sheet, laughing.

"You watch out, Lottie! We'll fix you, next time."

"Cousin Mary's Mammy will fix her if she finds that she has mussed her nice, white sheet," Jim said as he helped Lottie fold it.

"I've got to watch out," she told herself as she carried it back upstairs. "Jim will certainly try to help the other children find some way to give me my comeuppance."

Supper was every bit as good as she had expected it to be. There was hot Sally Lunn. There were sliced peaches and thick cream. The children, though, almost swallowed everything whole. They were anxious to get back to playing again. It wasn't long before they were running back to the yard.

"Now we can play Hiding!"

"Not It! Not It!"

"Let's count out. Lottie, you count!"

"All right." Lottie began to count.

> "Wire brier, limberlock,
> Ten geese in a flock.
> O-U-T spells out."

Cousin Jim was It. A big oak tree was home base. He leaned his head against it and closed his eyes. "I'll count five hundred by fives."

The children raced off. Lottie remembered a hollow place in the hedge by the sidewalk. It was close by Cousin Mary's thorn bush. Crouched inside, she was completely hidden. Jim went right past her. At last every one else had been caught, and he had to call "Home free for Lottie!"

She used the same hidey-hole the next time and the next, but when Jim was It again she was sure he had found her. He stopped back of the hedge, right by the fence post. The leaves were thin there. Surely he could see her white pinafore showing through in the moonlight. She did not dare to move. Why didn't he call out? What was he standing there for? She waited. Maybe he hadn't seen her after all. It seemed as if she crouched still for ages. At last Jim moved on.

"He almost got me!" Lottie chuckled to herself.

She started to peep to see if she could get back to home base. When she tried to move her head, something pulled it back. Her braid must have caught on a twig. She felt back. No, it wasn't caught. Why, it had been pulled through the hedge!

In a flash she knew what had happened. That Jim! He had seen her all right. He had pulled her braid through the hedge so carefully she hadn't even felt it. Then he had fastened it to the fence post. Probably he had used one of the thorns on the thorn bush. They were so long the servants often used them to fasten the wash on the line.

"Jim said he would give me my comeuppance and he has." Lottie wasn't angry. She felt it was only fair.

"Soon he'll call out 'Home free for Lottie!' and then how they'll all laugh when I try to get loose! But I'll fool them. I'll pretend not to hear, and when they come to laugh at me, I'll play like I'm asleep and don't even know my braid is pulled back."

It didn't pull while she stayed crouched down. The air was still and quiet. She might even have gone to sleep, sure enough, but just then some big boys came down the street outside the hedge. Even in the moonlight she could see that they were rough looking boys. Their voices were rough, too.

One of them was holding something in his hands. The others were doing something to it. It was giving pitiful little cries.

"Keep still! You'll have enough to cry about when we let you go."

"Hold him tight, Butch, while I fasten this knot."

"Scratch me, will you? Take that!"

There were more pitiful cries. Lottie peeped through the hedge. The boys had a cat. They were tying a tin pan to its tail.

Lottie forgot about her braid. She started forward. Her head pulled back with a sharp tug. Then she was free. Jim hadn't wanted really to hurt her. He hadn't pushed the thorn deep into the post. That short, sudden pull was all it needed to get her braid loose.

She didn't stop to figure that out. She went through the hedge like a cannon ball.

"You let that cat go!"

The boys were too startled to see that she was only a little girl.

"Give it to me!" She grabbed the cat. Pussy didn't wait to find out whether she was a rescuer or a new tormenter. He clawed deep.

"Ow!" Lottie let go. The cat made a dash for

"Hey! She let our cat go!"

the nearest tree. It climbed quickly to safety, high up in the branches.

"Hey! She let our cat go!"

"Grab *her*, then!"

"Pinch her!"

"Slap her!"

"Pull her hair!"

The boys were crowding around her now. They looked very big. Lottie looked very little. But she didn't back away an inch. She planted her two feet more firmly on the sidewalk.

"Yes, I let it go," she scolded. "You ought to be ashamed of yourselves, tormenting a poor helpless cat, big boys like you!"

"Huh!" Then, instead of slapping her, the biggest boy grinned. "She's a spunky little tyke, ain't she?"

The others began to grin, too.

"Aw, come on," said one of them. "It's getting late."

They started off down the street. Now the

other children in the yard came running. They had forgotten about Jim's trick, too.

"Did those boys hurt you?" Jim asked angrily.

Lottie shook her head. "But the cat did. I'll have to go get Mother to put some witch hazel on my arm where it scratched me."

"The mean thing!" one of the younger children cried. "I reckon now you're sorry you helped it."

"Indeed I'm not. It wasn't the cat's fault. It just didn't understand."

"Weren't you afraid?"

"Why, no." Lottie wasn't boasting. She was just stating a fact. "I don't believe I get afraid very often."

"Why not?"

"I don't know. Maybe it is because when something has to be done I get so busy doing it I haven't time to be afraid."

5
Sunday Dinner

THERE WAS a good deal of coming and going in the old home at Viewmont during the next two years.

"It is fine, sometimes," Lottie told Jim, "to have a large family, but then again, sometimes, it isn't. You always have to be telling somebody good-by. First it was Thomas going off to college. Then Uncle James and his family. Then Isaac. Now Orie is away at school."

"That leaves you Big Sister for the rest of the family, doesn't it?"

"Yes—and I don't like it a bit."

"Why not? You used to tell me you didn't like being Middle Sister a bit, either."

Lottie grinned. "I didn't. It seemed to me as if the older ones were always telling me what to do, and I always had to set a good example for the younger ones. No wonder I fussed! But now I guess I'm finding out that being Big Sister is a lot worse."

She sighed and then went on.

"Don't you remember how we all used to go to Orie with everything? 'Sister, I cut my finger!' 'Sister, I broke my doll. You fix it.' 'Sister, will you hear me say my lesson?' We thought she could do anything—and she just about could. But I can't."

"Give yourself time," Jim advised. "Don't you remember how you didn't like cooking at first? After a while, though, you thought it was fun."

"I still do, only I don't get a chance very often. Aunt Sukey is growing older and crosser every day. She says it bothers her to have 'young-uns' under foot in her kitchen."

"Then you'll just have to wait until she isn't there."

"And when will that be? Never. She comes up from her cabin to get breakfast before I am even awake, and I wake early. She stays until the fire is stone cold at night."

" 'Never' is a right long word."

"Um-hum," Lottie agreed and stopped. A sudden look of mischief flashed into her eyes. "Never—except on Sundays," she added.

Jim nodded. "That's right. Except on Sundays."

Both of them knew that Sunday was kept very carefully at Viewmont. The children mustn't study or sew. The servants mustn't work. Aunt Sukey kept a big fire going on Saturday. She fried chicken and cooked a ham. She made enough biscuit and light bread to last over Sunday. Mother made pies and cake. But on Sundays there was no fire in the kitchen. Aunt Sukey would go back to her cabin as soon as breakfast was over. When the Moon family came home from church they would have a cold dinner.

Even though there was preaching at the Scottsville church only two Sundays a month they had Sunday school there every Sunday. When the roads were so bad the horses couldn't get the carriage through, Mother would hold Sunday school for her family in their own parlor. That wasn't very often, though. Usually, dust or mud, rain or sun, the Moons went to Scottsville every Sunday morning.

But there was something very special about Mother. Lottie knew she could always depend on it. Mother not only expected her children to think for themselves as they grew older. She was willing to let them do it. But she would certainly be hurt if Lottie didn't want to go to Sunday school.

"And she'll probably pray about me," Lottie thought, uncomfortably, "but she won't say I *have* to go. And *will* she be surprised when she gets back home!"

"I'll have hot mashed potatoes," Lottie planned as she lay in bed that night, "with a deep place in the middle filled with melted butter. I'll have black-eyed peas and stewed tomatoes. And hot biscuit. Won't Father enjoy that? He doesn't like cold bread any better than I do."

But she was careful not to say anything to anyone else about her plans. When Sunday morning came, she waited until breakfast was nearly over.

"Now, children," Mother said in her usual brisk way, "don't dawdle. We must be ready to leave for Sunday school promptly."

Now that the time had actually come, Lottie felt her throat going dry. It took courage to stick to her plan, but stick to it she did.

"I'm not going," she said.

She hoped she didn't sound as excited as she felt. Not going! The other children looked at her in amazement.

"Why not?" asked her Father.

"Are you sick, Dear?" asked Mother, anxiously.

It would be easy to say she was sick. Then Mother wouldn't feel so hurt. But Lottie felt uncomfortable enough as it was. She certainly didn't want to have a fib on her conscience as well.

"No, ma'am, I'm not sick. I just don't feel like going to Sunday school this morning."

Mother looked at Father. Father looked at Mother. Would they say "You *must* go?" Father shook his head.

"You are old enough now to decide things for yourself," said Mother quietly, "but I am very disappointed."

Her lips closed in a tight line.

"I hope," Father added, "that you will change your mind before the carriage starts."

Lottie had no intention of changing her mind. She stayed in her room until the carriage drove off. She watched through the curtains as it disappeared in its own dust down the lane. There was no doubt about it. Even though she hadn't told a fib, her conscience hurt. Mother's shoulders drooped. After she got into the carriage she looked back. She was still hoping Lottie would come.

"But she always said," Lottie told herself, "that when the Lord gave me a mind of my own, he expected me to use it. And I am using it. I am going to do things my own way."

As soon as the carriage was out of sight she hurried across the yard to the kitchen. Aunt Sukey always left enough wood in the wood box to start the next fire. It was more work than she had expected to get the fire going but at last it began to blaze nicely. Now she must go to the garden for her vegetables.

Picking the tomatoes was easy but the black-eyed peas took more time. She hoped the fire wouldn't go out.

Back in the kitchen she bustled about as if she were Mother and Aunt Sukey and herself rolled into one. Everything must be ready before the family returned.

It was. There was a broad smudge across the cook's face. She had a bad burn on her wrist. But when the carriage turned into the lane she was ready to start "dishing up."

Mother came hurrying to the kitchen door the moment the horses stopped. She had seen the smoke coming from the chimney. She was startled. Smoke from the kitchen chimney on Sunday!

"Lottie! What in the world has happened?"

Lottie was bending over the oven. She was taking the hot biscuit out. They were as light and brown as any Aunt Sukey had ever made. She turned to Mother with a mischievous twinkle in her eye.

"Hurry up and take off your things, Mother, while I ring the bell. Dinner is ready."

It wasn't a happy dinner. Father sat stiff and disapproving. Mother looked as if every mouthful hurt her. Only the children enjoyed it. But even they were very quiet as they looked at Father and Mother. Lottie was glad when it was over.

She was glad, too, that the dishwashing could wait over until Monday. That was one way of keeping the sabbath to which she had no objection. And wouldn't Aunt Sukey be furious when she saw her kitchen!

"Lottie! What in the world has happened?"

"I'll have to give her something extra nice to make up for it," Lottie decided. "I'll use the money I was saving for new gloves to buy her some earrings."

"You must be tired, Lottie," Mother said as they rose from the table. "Suppose you go to your room for the afternoon."

Lottie wasn't sure whether Mother meant just what she said, or whether she was sending her to her room for punishment as if she were a little girl. But there was no doubt about it—she was tired. She went to the room she shared with her sisters and threw herself down on the bed. Then she got up again. It would never do for the little girls to find that Big Sister had lain down without taking off her dress.

"I've set them a bad enough example as it is," she thought drearily.

But the little girls didn't come up. Mother must have told them to take their naps in her room or on the big sofa in the hall.

"Probably she wants to have a serious talk with me, by herself," Lottie decided. How she dreaded Mother's "serious talks"!

But Mother didn't come up either. "She must want me to think things through by myself. Good. I've thought them through. And I still don't believe it is wrong to make up the kitchen fire on Sunday."

Deep down, Lottie knew she wasn't being honest with herself. Making up the fire wasn't the real trouble. Having her own way when she knew it would make Mother unhappy—that was the root of the whole thing.

"I suppose it really boils down to the fact that I am selfish. Then isn't Mother selfish, too, to want things done *her* way?" Lottie thought about that for a while.

"No," she decided at last. "Mother isn't selfish. She just wants to do what she thinks is right, and I want to do what I think is fun."

She wriggled uncomfortably on the bed. "**Why**

can't I think as she does? Maybe it is just because I am young. No, that's not the real answer. Mother has something deep inside her that I haven't got. What is it?"

6

April Fool!

Lottie had always known that some day she
would go away to school. All of the older children
had gone. She had always thought it would be
fun, but when the time actually came, she wasn't
sure.

It was a long trip over the mountains to the
Virginia Female Seminary. The stagecoach
bounced and jolted along the rocky roads. Miles
before they reached the school fourteen-year-old
Lottie was homesick. Would Sarah take care of
her flowers? Would Shep miss her? Would Baby

Edmonia remember her when she came home at Christmas?

Other questions kept pushing into her thoughts, too. She had never met so many new girls before in all her life. Would she like them? Would they like her? The more she worried the more miserable she became.

At last the coach rounded a long bend in the road. Ahead of them were two large buildings with a walk that ran in a circle between them.

"Yonder is the Virginia Female Seminary," one of the passengers told her.

Lottie swallowed hard to keep back her tears. If only she could turn around and go home! But what would Mother say to that? In fact, what would she say to herself if she did such a foolish thing?

She bit her lips together to keep them from trembling. She threw her braid back over her shoulder. She would show herself whether she was a homesick crybaby or not! When the coach stopped in front of the Seminary she was ready.

"Hello!" she said under her breath to the big buildings. "Here I come!"

Suddenly the buildings almost seemed to smile back at her.

"Why," thought Lottie in surprise. "I may even grow to like it here!"

She did. Before the first week was up she was glad she hadn't gone home. Meeting the new girls wasn't hard at all. Emma, Letty, Carey Ann— she knew she could be friends with them all.

At night, after the candles were out, she would still cry a few tears into her pillow when she thought about home. But there were curious little noises in the room. She was pretty sure her roommates were crying into their pillows too. Somehow, that made her feel better. Then, soon, all of them were too busy for tears.

Latin! French! Algebra! Arithmetic! Natural science! English composition! There didn't seem to be any end to the books piled on the tables by

"Hello! Here I come!"

their beds. There didn't seem to be any end to the studying that had to be done either.

Dong! went the big bell in the belfry over the attic. It waked them at six in the morning. Dong! It called them to worship. Dong! Dong! to breakfast. Dong! to classes. Not until four o'clock was there a minute Lottie could call her own.

From four until supper time she could do as she pleased. Some of the girls would spend the time writing letters. Some would go to their rooms for a little sewing, or mending. Not Lottie! She had more exciting things to do. Sometimes she would go down to the big room in the basement to dance a Virginia reel. She would go out to the kitchen to tease the cook for some gingerbread. She might even slip through the gate for a forbidden ramble down the country road.

Whatever she did, it seemed almost no time before—Dong! Dong! The bell called them to study hour.

"It's bad enough to have teachers telling us what to do all the time," Lottie grumbled to Carey Ann, "but it's worse still to be ordered around all day by a *bell.*"

When she settled down by her candlestand, though, with her algebra and her Latin grammar, she wasn't at all unhappy. In fact, as time went on, she found she really liked to study. Mother had every reason to be satisfied with the reports that went home, so far as grades were concerned. But when it came to "deportment"—that was quite different.

"I just don't see the sense in having so many

rules," Lottie told Carey Ann. "What difference does it make *when* I get up? Or *when* I go to bed? Or whether I get to breakfast exactly on time? At home, just so long as I behaved myself I could do as I pleased."

"I should think you would like having rules," Carey Ann teased, "because the more there are, the more you can break. I've never seen a girl enjoy breaking rules as much as you do."

Lottie laughed. "Maybe you're right. But at home—"

Dong! Dong! went the bell. Recreation hour was over.

Lottie looked up at the belfry tower.

"Some day I am going to do something to that bell," she said.

"What?"

"I don't know yet, but just you wait and see."

Of course there was no rush about it. She had become a member of one of the literary societies. She was helping edit its school paper. She was taking part in the special exercises which came at the end of every week. There really wasn't time to plan a big prank right now. But she couldn't keep out of mischief altogether.

"It's when she looks so very innocent that you have to watch out for her," Lou Belle giggled to her roommate. "Look at her now! She's walking around the lawn with Letty as prim as a plaster saint, but it is more than likely that she is cooking up some new trick to play on us."

She was. "The workmen are plastering the laundry room wall," Lottie was telling Letty, "and there is a big sand pile down there. It is lovely coarse sand. I'm going to get me a cupful. Then you keep Lou Belle talking downstairs while I sprinkle sand between her sheets. Maybe I'll sprinkle Janie Sue's, too."

"Don't you dare touch mine," said Letty. "It would be just like you to pretend I was in on the joke and then play it on me."

"I wish I had thought of it."

"What are you two talking about?" Lou Belle stopped on the walkway in front of them.

"We were talking about sand," said Lottie very truthfully. "Have you ever thought about all the ways you can use it? Folks make plaster with it, or glass, or garden walks, or—"

"I don't see anything in that to giggle about the way you were doing."

"What were *you* talking about?" Lottie changed the subject quickly.

"About the way so many girls nowadays use their middle names. It is Carey Ann and Lou Belle and Janie Sue and ever so many others. You don't ever use yours, though, do you? 'Lottie D. Moon.' What does the 'D' stand for?"

"Devil," said Lottie promptly. Her eyes twinkled. "Don't you think it fits?"

That night, when Lou Belle found her sheets sprinkled with scratching sand, she certainly did.

It wasn't until spring that Lottie finally made up her mind what to do about the bell. The idea came

suddenly. It was a beautiful morning at the end
of March. A red bird was singing in the tree outside her window. Lottie decided she was tired of
studying. With her finger marking her place in
her book, she watched the bird fly from branch to
branch. Her eyes grew dreamy. She wondered
if—

Dong! Dong!

She was so startled she dropped her book.

"Wake up, honey!" laughed Emma.

"I have," said Lottie. "And, what is more, I
waked up with an idea."

She thought about her idea all through the
day.

"I can use my old sheets," she planned. "And
there is my extra blanket. I don't need that, now
the nights are warmer."

She told no one about her plan. It would be
fun to surprise them. That night she dropped off
to sleep saying to herself, "You must wake up
early—very, very early."

She did. There were only a few faint bird chirpings in the trees outside. The dawn was still grey in the east.

Very quietly she crept out of bed and quickly slipped into her clothes. She gathered up the sheets and blankets she had left on her chair the night before. Then she tiptoed across the room and opened the door carefully. She looked back. Her roommates had not waked. Good!

The steps to the attic were steep and narrow. The belfry above wasn't even floored. She walked the rafters carefully until she reached the ladder up to the big bell. In the dim light it looked steep and dangerous. But who was afraid of a ladder? Certainly not a girl who had climbed just about every tree in the yard at Viewmont.

She tied a stout cord around her bundle, with one end as long as the ladder itself. Then, leaving the bundle on the rafters, but keeping one end of the cord in her hand, she climbed until she reached the bell. Next she pulled the bundle up.

"Now let's hear how loud you can ring!"

Carefully, she wrapped the sheets and towels around the clapper of the big bell. She tied them with the cord. There! Leaning back against the ladder, she looked at her work.

"Now let's hear how loud you can ring."

It took only a few moments to climb down the ladder. She crossed the rafters and hurried down the stairs to her room. Her roommates were still

sleeping soundly as Lottie slipped quietly back
into bed.

No rising bell rang at six o'clock that morning
at the Virginia Female Seminary. The girls slept
on—all but Lottie. Now that she had the chance
she couldn't sleep. She watched the sunbeams
push farther and farther across the window sill.
She wondered whether the old janitor had found

She hurried down the ladder.

out yet why the bell didn't ring. She wondered if he had called the principal. She wondered if the batter bread for breakfast would be burned to a crisp before the girls waked. She wondered—

Dong! Dong!

The sudden clang startled her so she nearly fell out of bed. She was almost glad to hear it.

Roll call was over an hour late that morning. The principal was very serious.

"Someone," he told the girls, "has robbed each of you this morning of a precious hour. I shall expect the thief to come to my office immediately after breakfast."

How the girls buzzed and whispered! It was easy to guess what had happened. More than one of them looked at Lottie. It was just such a trick as she would love to play. But now, would she confess?

They needn't have worried. Lottie had had her fun. Now she was ready to pay for it. As soon as breakfast was over, she flung her braid back over her shoulder. With her head high she went to the principal's office.

The girls stood in little groups in the hall. Some of them giggled nervously. Some of them whispered together. How did she ever dare climb that ladder? What would happen to her now?

At last she came out. Her head was still high.

"Lottie!" They crowded around her. "Are you going to be sent home?"

She shook her head. "But that is about the only thing that isn't going to happen to me. My grade on 'deportment' on my next report is going to be just about zero. And my recreation hours are taken away from now until kingdom come." For a moment she looked serious. Then she chuckled. "But it was fun."

7
Two Ways Come Together

"THE NICEST thing about going away is coming home."

Lottie was sitting in a low chair while Mammy brushed her hair. "It's good to have you take care of me again, Mammy. At school I had to do everything for myself."

Little Edmonia was building a paper doll house on the floor. She looked up at her big sister. "I don't see how you ever had time to. But maybe you weren't as busy at school as you are here at home."

"Goodness me! I was ever so much busier! I studied morning, noon, and night. Now I am just resting up."

"Resting!" said Mammy. "Humph! Parties! Company! Dining days! Hayrides! You're getting just about as much rest as a hummingbird!"

"Well, of course, there *is* quite a bit going on right now, while Cousin Jim and Carey Ann are getting married. Things will quiet down after that, though."

"Maybe," grumbled Mammy. "Then again, maybe they won't. What with getting Miss Orie ready to go to France—"

"It is *Doctor* Orie now, Mammy," Lottie corrected. "Aren't you proud to have a woman doctor in the family?"

Mammy shook her head. "I'd lots rather see her get married and settle down, the way a young lady ought to do. And you, too."

Lottie groaned.

"Please, Mammy, not yet. I haven't been a

young lady very long. Give me a little time."

"Give you time and you'll go traipsing off to school again, just the way Miss Orie did."

"Well, not *just* the same way. I promise you I won't study medicine."

Edmonia left her doll house and came over to stand by her big sister. "You won't go away again right away, will you, Lottie? You said you would show me how to make cornshuck doll babies."

Lottie hugged her little sister.

"Of course I shall, honey. Just wait until things quiet down. We're going to have a good time together."

It seemed to Edmonia that Lottie was right. During the quiet weeks that came after Cousin Jim and Carey Ann were married and the company was gone, the little girl thought they had a very good time. Her sister, though, wasn't so sure.

There was something wrong with Lottie. "But I don't know what it is," she thought crossly.

"What makes me so restless and uneasy all the time? Nothing satisfies me nowadays."

She watched her mother. Mrs. Moon wasn't restless or unhappy. Goodness! She didn't have time to be. Ever since Father had died, nearly five years ago, Mother had taken care of the house, the farm, the store—everything! But it wasn't all of her work which kept that quiet, happy look in her eyes. Lottie began to ask herself the same question she had asked years ago. "What has Mother got that I don't have?"

Deep down in her heart she knew the answer, but she wasn't willing to admit it. Mother was a Christian.

"But I don't want to be a Christian. I want to live my life my own way. It is *my* life," Lottie fumed.

"I've rested enough now," she told Mammy. "It's time for me to get ready for school again."

"School!" scolded Mammy. "You've had too much schooling already."

Lottie knew most of Mother's friends felt the same way. It was all right for boys to go to school and to college, but girls? No. If a girl could read and write and count, what more did she need? Of course, if her parents could afford it, a little French was all right and maybe a few piano lessons. She might even learn to draw and paint a bit, too. By the time a girl was seventeen, though, she was certainly old enough to stop school and get married.

When Orianna became a doctor the neighbors were shocked. Now Lottie was going to do something almost as unusual. She was going to a school in Charlottesville where they taught young women exactly the same things the boys were studying at the University close by. Latin! Greek! How ridiculous!

Lottie was glad Mother didn't think it was ridiculous. For a while, after she started at the Albemarle Female Institute she was so busy she forgot the restless, unsatisfied feeling.

It wasn't for very long, though. There were girls at the school who were like Mother. They were happy just as Mother was and for the same reason. Just to watch them made Lottie feel cross. She began to play jokes on them. She teased them, just to show how smart she really was.

"You believe whatever your parents believed," she told them. "Now look at me. *I* always think things out for myself."

One Sunday morning, while the other girls dressed for church, Lottie slipped away from the school. There was a big book under her arm. Outside the town a path led through the fields. The Indian summer sun shone down from a blue sky. Church bells began to ring.

"Who cares?" Lottie asked herself. "Certainly I don't."

As the bells died away she came to a big haystack.

"Now this," she said happily, "is just what I have been looking for."

She dropped down against the hay. Then she

wriggled and twisted until she had made herself a warm, comfortable hollow. She opened her book. In a tree nearby, a squirrel began to scold. Lottie laughed.

"If you're fussing at me," she said, "you're wrong. I am reading Shakespeare. It is ever so much better than a dry sermon would be in church. And there is no need to say that maybe the sermon wouldn't have been dry," she added. "I'd just rather be here anyway."

But somehow, she couldn't enjoy Shakespeare as much as she usually did.

It was in the spring of the next year that special revival services were held at the school. Many of the girls went to every meeting.

"Won't you come along with us?" they asked Lottie.

She shook her head. Her hand went up to toss her braid back over her shoulder, but she was a young lady now, and her braids were pinned securely at the back of her head. Instead, she fingered

"I'd rather be here anyway."

the little earring in her ear as she shook her head more positively than ever.

One of the girls looked relieved. "It is just as well," she said. "If you come, you'd only make fun of everything, and that hurts. I know you are wrong, but I don't know how to prove it. If you weren't so bright, Lottie—only you aren't, really, you know, because you are bright the wrong way."

Lottie felt more uncomfortable than ever as she watched the girls go off without her. She didn't really want to hurt anyone.

"The truth is," she thought in a puzzled way, "it is myself I want to hurt. Oh, why do I have to be so mixed up inside about everything?"

The girl had given her an idea, though. "I *shall* go to the meeting. I can tease the others a lot more if I know exactly what the preacher says."

And to the meeting she went. As soon as it was over the girls hurried to their rooms. They were holding a sunrise meeting in the morning. If they didn't get to bed promptly, they wouldn't wake in time.

Lottie hurried to her room, too. There had been nothing in the sermon at which she could poke fun. Instead, it had made her more dissatisfied with herself than ever.

"I can't go on like this," she told herself. "To-night, by myself, I am going to think this through."

"But not by myself," the thought came from deep within her. "I know what Mother would say. 'Think—and pray.'"

It was a long night. No one but Lottie ever

knew exactly what happened. But something did happen. Did Lottie's awareness of Christ come suddenly, like a blinding light, as it had to Saul on the way to Damascus? Or, like Elijah, did she hear Him in a still small voice? She never told anyone. But the next morning Lottie went to the sunrise service.

"Oh dear," whispered the youngest girl when she came in. "I'll never be able to pray in front of her—never! I'll be absolutely tongue-tied."

This, though, was a new Lottie. No one needed to be tongue-tied before her.

"May I join you?" she asked quietly. When the girls hesitated in surprise, Lottie added, "I've changed. I have given myself to Christ. His way is my way, now."

8
War Time

LOTTIE WAS no Indian giver. Nor did she ever do things halfway. When she gave herself to Christ she gave her whole self. It was "for keeps."

She was quite sensible about it, though. Christ's way was now her own way. Where would it lead her? She didn't expect the answer in a blinding flash. Would he want her to be a doctor as Orie was? Would he want her to be a teacher? He had called Mother to be a Christian wife and mother. With a stir of excitement she remembered the story of Ann Hasseltine Judson. Just suppose—

But there was no time now to "just suppose." Whatever he wanted her to do, she must be ready. The first step in getting ready was to finish school. The days seemed to go by just as they had before, but there was a difference.

"I'm not afraid of Lottie any more," the youngest girl told her roommate. "Her tongue is as quick as ever but it isn't sharp."

"I know. She doesn't laugh *at* us any more. She laughs *with* us."

Neither of them knew how hard Lottie was finding it to do just that. It was much easier, she learned, to make smart, mean remarks, than smart, kind ones. God had given her a quick mind. To be patient with those who were slower than she was, to help instead of to tease—that was her first lesson. It was almost her hardest lesson. But hard lessons had never frightened Lottie.

As the last weeks of school drew near, a new tense feeling of excitement filled the air. War! At first it didn't seem too horrible. There was something thrilling and romantic about it. The boys looked so handsome in their new grey uniforms. Of course they wouldn't be gone long. The South would win and then—

Lottie smiled to herself. There was a young professor at the University. As soon as college closed he was joining the army as a chaplain. Before he left for camp, though, Mother had invited him to visit at Viewmont.

Ever so many of Lottie's friends were becoming engaged to soldiers. She smiled to herself again as she snipped her thread. She was sewing white stars on a blue background. It was part of a flag which the girls were making together. Now one of them stopped her own work to admire Lottie's.

"My goodness! What tiny, even stitches you make. Your great-grandmother, herself, couldn't have sewn a finer seam."

"It isn't fair for one girl to be able to do everything so well, the way Lottie does," another spoke up. "Sewing, cooking, Latin, Greek, French."

"There is a certain young professor not so many miles from here who doesn't care a rap for all that. He just wants her to be able to say, in English, one three-letter word."

Lottie blushed. "You are perfect geese, all of you." But she was still smiling as she folded her work and put on her bonnet to go to class.

Commencement was over. Lottie was now a Master of Arts. Her school days were over too. She was ready for—what? She didn't know.

There were busy days ahead of her at Viewmont. Sarah and Mary were back from school, too, for the summer, and Dr. Orie was home from abroad. Uncle James and his family were at home, too. And among the house guests was the young preacher. Even with all this coming and going, though, Lottie found time to think and to pray. Quietly she decided that she could not tell the young professor that "little three-letter word."

If she wasn't going to get married, what was she

going to do? The answer to that question during those first years was easy: "Help Mother."

Of course Orie was Big Sister. If she could have stayed home she would have been Mother's chief helper. But the army needed doctors and Orie was a doctor. It wasn't long before she had to go. But even in her short stay with them, Lottie grew to know her big sister better than she ever had before. There was a bond, now, that drew them together. They didn't need to talk about it any more than they needed to talk about how much they loved Mother, but it was there. Orie, too, had given her heart and life to Christ.

"After studying in the hospitals in Paris I went to Jerusalem to visit Uncle James," she told Lottie. "Oh, the work there was for a doctor to do there! I couldn't help but pitch in and then, well—I felt God call me."

Edmonia was listening, too. "It is a good feeling, isn't it?" she asked.

Her older sisters looked at each other and smiled.

"Yes," said Orie, "it is a good feeling."

"What kinds of sick folk did you cure in Jerusalem?"

"Oh, all kinds. But I worked mostly with people with sore eyes." Then Orie burst out laughing.

"What is funny?"

"There was an old Arab chief I helped once. And when he thanked me, he gave me the Arab blessing: he hoped I would have as many children as the stars in the sky, but none of them girls."

"Why, the idea!" Edmonia was indignant. "I'm glad I am a girl. There are ever so many things we girls can do."

"She is certainly right about that," Lottie thought. "There is work, work, work!"

Soon she found out there were many things harder than work. The war was coming closer. Word came that there had been a big battle at Manassas. The wounded were being brought to Charlottesville. They were using the University buildings for hospitals. They needed nurses.

Lottie hurried to Charlottesville. So did Sarah and Mary. There they soon found that war was

War was not at all romantic.

not at all romantic. It was terrible. There weren't enough medicines or bandages or anything. There was only suffering and death. It was a very sober Lottie who returned to Viewmont when her help was no longer needed with the wounded.

"Did you see Orie while you were there?" her anxious mother asked.

"Indeed, yes. She was here, there, and everywhere. There was a young Dr. Andrews there, too. His brother was badly wounded. He and Orie were working over the boy together."

It was terrible.

"Did they save him?"

Lottie shook her head sadly. "No. But they learned to know each other very well while they were trying to. I shouldn't wonder, Mother, but what we'll soon have another doctor in our family."

"I would be glad for Orie," said her mother.

July and August came and went. When crisp September arrived it seemed strange not to be going back to school.

"I'm not even a young girl any longer," thought Lottie. She stood before a mirror putting on her earrings. "I'm a woman. And Edmonia isn't a child any longer, either. She is a young girl. She is really the one who should be going off to school."

But there were very few schools open now. And even if there was a school, there was no way to get there, and no money to pay her fees.

"I wonder, Lottie," said Mother, "if you couldn't teach Edmonia an hour or two every day."

"Why, of course," Lottie agreed. She brought down from the storeroom the books she had used at the Seminary. Soon the one-teacher, one-pupil school was under way. Almost at once, she found that this was no burden at all. Edmonia was a quick learner. Soon she was sharing with Lottie all the studies, the poetry, the books which Lottie loved best.

"School is doing me every bit as much good as it is Edmonia," she said one day to Mrs. Moon. "You know, I believe I could be a teacher."

The sisters were busy with their books one morning when Old Tom, one of the Negro field workers came running down the road. "Miss Ann M'ria!" he called to Mrs. Moon. "Miss Ann M'ria!"

When Mrs. Moon came rushing to the door Tom was almost too breathless to say another word. He stood there trembling all over. The house servants crowded around him. Edmonia dropped her slate. Lottie rushed out, too.

"The soldiers a'coming! They burn Charlottes-ville now. Marse Jim's old home is ablazing. They're going t' be here 'most any minute!"

"Catch your breath," said Mother quietly. "I don't see any dust up the road yet. Are you *sure* they are coming?"

"Yes, ma'am. Sure, pos'tive."

Mother looked at Lottie. They knew that the Northern troops were at Winchester. The soldiers had once made a raid down as far as New Market. It might very well be true that they were coming down the valley now.

"Mammy," said Mrs. Moon. "Go tell the boys

to get the cows and hide them down in the woods by the river. We'd better hide the horses and mules, too."

Lottie was already starting for the sideboard. "Get me an old tablecloth, please, Edmonia, and help me wrap up the silver."

They made two bundles of it. "We'll go to the orchard," said Lottie, "and bury them under one of the apple trees. No, we'd better bury them in two places. Then, if the soldiers find one, they'll think that is all there is."

"How about that big old tree yonder for one of them?"

"No. That is too easy to recognize. We'll choose trees that look just like all the others. Then we'll make a secret mark, so that we can recognize them ourselves."

Lottie had brought the fire shovel from the kitchen. Now she began to dig a big hole beneath one of the very ordinary looking trees in the apple orchard. There she and Edmonia buried one of the bundles. When the place was carefully covered again with leaves, she made two small cuts near the bottom of the tree.

"Now for the other bundle. Keep an eye on the road, honey, while I dig," she said.

She chose another ordinary looking tree and began to dig near its trunk.

"Hurry, oh, hurry, Lottie!" urged Edmonia as she strained to see far down the road.

She began to dig a big hole.

"I am! Fast as I can." Lottie's breath was short.

Just as she had finished her task, one of the servants came running.

"Yonder they come!" he cried. "Yonder they come!"

Far up the road they could see a cloud of dust.

"Quick!" cried Lottie. "They mustn't see us anywhere near the orchard or they'd suspect."

She caught Edmonia's hand and they ran toward the house, the servant following right behind them.

The cloud of dust drew nearer. The little group standing at the door could see through it now. It wasn't soldiers at all—just an old man driving a flock of sheep to safety in Scottsville!

The Moons waited anxiously all that day and the next. Still there were no soldiers. At last a man came down the road from Charlottesville.

"Why, no," he told them. "The city hasn't been burned, or Monticello either. That was just one of those rumors."

Mother sent the boys down to the woods to

bring back the cattle. Lottie and Edmonia went back to the orchard with their fire shovel. They found the first tree easily and dug up the bundle.

"Now," said Lottie straightening up, "let's get the other one."

They had passed several trees when Lottie suddenly stopped short. Her hand flew to her mouth and her eyes had a horrified look in them.

"Edmonia," she said in a small scared voice. "I didn't mark that tree!" Only then did they realize that, in their hurry when Old Tom came they had just picked up their shovels and run.

They dug first under one tree, then under another, but the second bundle was never found.

"Maybe the soldiers *did* come and find it," one of the servants suggested.

"Maybe," Lottie said doubtfully.

"Or maybe," Edmonia suggested, "one of our grandchildren will find it some day."

"Maybe," Lottie agreed again.

"Only it would be nicer if we could find it our-selves."

This time Lottie agreed without any "maybe." But they never did.

9
Miss Moon, Schoolmistress

THERE was no use in crying over spilt milk. Besides, there wasn't time. The end of the war was drawing near. It was a sad ending for the people of the South. So many of their men had been killed; so many homes had been burned. And the cause for which they had fought was lost!

People had said Grandfather was the richest man in the county. Now Mrs. Moon had to sell one part of the plantation after another to make ends meet. People had said, too, that it was silly for her to educate her girls so that they could earn their own living. But Lottie was very glad that she had.

Orie had married the young army doctor. Mary and Sarah were married, too, and did not live at Viewmont any longer. Isaac was a young man now. He could help Mother run the farm better than Lottie could. And Edmonia could help. She was almost a young lady.

That meant that Lottie was free to do what she could. But where should she go? What should she do? She remembered her one-pupil school with Edmonia.

"The South needs teachers," she told herself. Soon she was starting a school in the home of some friends in Alabama.

It was a long way from Viewmont. She looked forward as anxiously as a school girl to letters from home. The oldest boy in the house would ride to town for the family mail bag. Then everyone would gather in the hall while it was being opened.

"Let's see. There is one for you, Mother; two

for Father; and here is one for Miss Lotte Moon."

Lottie reached out her hand eagerly.

"But it isn't for you," he teased. "It is for L-o-t-t-e. Your name is L-o-t-t-i-e."

"My name isn't really either," said Lottie. "It is Charlotte."

"I never heard anyone call you that."

"They never do. It was such a grown-up name for a baby child that it was shortened to Lotte while I was in long baby clothes."

"Then how did it get to be Lottie?"

"Oh, the two names were so much alike folks just got them mixed up."

"Don't you mind? I know a woman named Jayne who is always getting upset when people spell it Jane."

"It doesn't bother me a bit. Don't you remember, Shakespeare said 'What's in a name?'"

The boy nodded. "I suppose he meant that it doesn't matter how your name is spelled. It is yourself that counts."

"Something like that," Lottie answered briskly. "I agree with him. I'm beginning to sign myself just 'L. Moon.' Then no one has to worry about the spelling. It saves time, too. Now, please, may I have my letter?"

He handed it to her. Lottie started to break the seal. Then she looked up in surprise. "Why, it isn't from Mother. It is postmarked Kentucky. Who on earth is writing me from way out there?"

"You could open it and see," the boy suggested with a grin.

Lottie laughed, too. "That might be a good idea," she admitted.

She took one of the hairpins that held her braid coiled around her head and slit the envelope carefully. "It is from the pastor of the Baptist church at Danville. He wants me to come out there to teach and help him with his church work."

"But we don't want you to leave us."

"I don't want to leave. Still—"

"I suppose you have to practice what you preach.

And you are always telling us we must do whatever helps people in the most ways. Only," Lottie's young student added, "I have found out that thing is usually the most work, too."

Lottie found out that he was right as soon as she reached Danville. She worked harder than ever before. She enjoyed it, though, and she made new friends, too. There was Miss Safford, who taught in the school with her. The two young women found they could work very well together.

It wasn't long before they received an invitation to come to Georgia and start a school at Cartersville. Starting a new school wasn't easy. Who cared? That made it all the more interesting. As soon as they reached Cartersville the two young women set to work. They found a building. They got their schoolrooms ready. They planned the studies the girls were to take. They talked to parents. They talked to girls. Finally the school opened. From the very beginning it was a success.

Now Lottie found time for a few other things.

She began to teach a Sunday school class. Soon she was visiting in the homes of her scholars.

"We missed Janey Lou last Sunday," she told one little girl's mother. "I hope she wasn't sick."

"No'm. Janey Lou, she almost never gets sick. But that poor child just hasn't got any clothes fit to wear into the Lord's house."

"The Lord isn't interested in her clothes."

"No'm, but the other children are. Besides, the weather was so raw and cold that if she had started traipsing around without a coat she'd have caught her death of cold."

Lottie looked around the bare little room. She looked at the mother's clothes. They were worn and patched.

"We'll have to see what we can do about it," she said quietly.

Back in her own room she counted the money she had saved from her last month's salary.

"There is just about enough to buy the cloth for a good warm coat. But how can I squeeze in the time to make it? Well, at least I can try."

"I'll help," Miss Safford offered. "If only we had one of those sewing machines we hear so much about!"

"That would be mighty nice. But I'm thankful we don't have to weave the cloth the way our mothers used to do."

During the long winter evenings, after their school work for the next day was planned, the two young women would sit and sew. As they sewed, they talked. They talked about the hard times, about their plans, about the books they had read.

"Did you ever hear of Mrs. Ann Hasseltine Judson?" Lottie asked one evening.

Miss Safford nodded.

"Mother read us a book about her when I was a child. And I am just as thrilled now as I was then whenever I think of the work she did in Burmah."

"Of course," said Miss Safford, "there are other places that need missionaries."

"I know. My uncle went to Palestine."

"And then, there is China. There must be such a lot of work to do there."

For a while neither of them spoke. The clock on the wall ticked loudly.

"Yes," said Lottie at last, thoughtfully. "There is China."

Janey Lou was delighted with her coat. And when warm weather came, Lottie had a spring dress ready. "Miss Lottie," Janey Lou told her friends, "certainly can do a lot of things besides talk."

But neither Janey Lou nor any one else knew about all of the things Lottie was doing. No wonder she never had any time or money to spend on herself! There were other poor children in town who needed clothes and sometimes even food. People soon found out that whenever they tried to collect money for some good purpose they could always depend on Lottie for a contribution. Beside all of this, she and Edmonia were supporting a little girl in a mission school in China. Forty-five dollars a year in gold! That took a big bite out of her savings.

In all of this giving she had one firm rule. Her

name mustn't be mentioned. It wasn't the giver that counted. It was the gift. "If you acknowledge receipt of this in print, please don't put my name." It was a request she was to make many times during her life. "Just say it is from Albemarle County" or "Just say it is from Virginia." No one ever knew how very much L. Moon was giving.

Janey Lou was delighted with her coat.

Late that spring Mrs. Moon became ill. Lottie hurried home to nurse her, but there was little she could do. Before many days her sister Orie received a letter. "Mother went home to God today, about two o'clock."

Summer vacation had started. Lottie stayed on at Viewmont for a while to help Isaac and Edmonia. How strange it seemed to find them both grown up! But Edmonia still remembered the days when Lottie had been her teacher. She still felt as her big sister did about many things, but in some ways she had gone even farther than Lottie. Lottie was still not yet quite sure about how she should spend the rest of her life. Edmonia was certain. She had already decided to be a missionary to China.

During the next two years Lottie was as busy as ever. The school grew. She knew that the people in Cartersville liked her. To know that she was both useful and popular, she felt, ought to be enough to make her happy, but it wasn't.

Edmonia had arrived in China. She was busy learning the Chinese language. "I always like studying a new language," Lottie remembered, reading her sister's letters about the funny mistakes she made in Chinese. "I wonder if Chinese is any harder than Greek."

"How about her housekeeping?" asked Miss Safford. "Can your sister make people understand what she wants done?" Miss Safford was almost as interested in Edmonia's letters as Lottie was.

So were Janey Lou and her other Sunday school girls. "Tell us what Miss Edmonia is doing," they begged every Sunday.

Lottie was almost sure now that she wanted to join Edmonia. "But I must be more than *almost* sure," she told herself. "I must be very, *very* sure."

At last there came a Sunday morning in February that seemed like any other Sunday morning. She taught her class as usual. She met Miss Safford in their usual pew for the church service. There was the usual rustle of folks settling in their places after the hymn. The minister read his text: "Lift up your eyes and look upon the fields for they are ripe already unto harvest."

As he spoke, Lottie Moon felt her last doubts slip away. This was the call for which she had been waiting. When the sermon was over she looked at Miss Safford. Miss Safford looked at her. Together they walked down the church aisle.

"We are ready," they said to the minister.

10

The New Railroad

WE'RE on our way; we're on our way!" the train
wheels clacked happily.

"Look!" cried the little boy jumping up and
down in the seat behind Lottie's. "Look quick!
That prairie dog turned a somersault. Honest, he
did!"

Lottie Moon turned to the window as excited
as the little boy.

"You're just a child, Lottie Moon," Miss Safford
laughed. "Who would ever think you're over
thirty years old?"

Lottie laughed too. "Of course I'm excited. Aren't you? Prairie dogs! Indians! Buffaloes! Gold mines! Antelope steak for dinner!"

"And don't forget you'll eat that dinner over a hundred miles from where you ate breakfast. Isn't that exciting, too?"

"It is, indeed. I know twenty-two miles an hour isn't really fast. Some of the trains back East go much faster. But, all the same, we'll be in San Francisco in less than two weeks from the time we left home. Ten years ago, by stagecoach, it would have taken us two months just to get there from Missouri."

"And to go from Virginia by boat would have taken over eight months!"

The little boy behind them had climbed down from his seat. Now he was climbing up by Lottie. Children always liked her. Maybe it was because she always liked children. She had made friends with this little fellow by telling him stories on the long journey.

"Tell me a story," he begged. "Tell me about how they built this railroad."

"Well," began Lottie, "let's see. How old are you?"

"I'm going on seven."

"Then you are a good bit older than our railroad. It won't be five until next spring."

The little boy grinned. To be older than a railroad was enough to make anyone feel big.

"Five years ago," Lottie kept on with her story, "over ten thousand men were working to lay the tracks on this side of the mountains. And ten thousand men were working on the other side. They had to build bridges and tunnels. They had to cut through the mountains. Sometimes half the men had to fight off the Indians while the other half worked. Sometimes they had to dig deep down under the snow to reach the ground on which to lay the rails.

"Finally, the day came when the men working on the west track could see the men working on the east track. Then the two tracks were joined. The last rail was laid. They used two silver and one gold spike to fasten it down.

" 'Clang! Clang!' went the hammer.

" 'Clickety, clickety, click!' went the telegraph machines all over the country. They were telling the great news. The railroad was finished! The Atlantic and the Pacific oceans were joined together by two thin iron rails."

The little boy wriggled happily. "So now I can go all the way on the steam cars to see my father again," he said. "He is building a new home out West for my mama and me. He sent for us last month. Where are you going?"

The train began to slow down for the dinner stop. The little boy's mother called him.

"Come, Son. It's time to wash your face and tidy up a bit."

Lottie reached for her bonnet. She wanted to freshen herself a little, too. She smiled as the little boy started down the aisle with his mother.

"I am just like him," she thought to herself. "I am on my way to the new home my Father has for me, too."

The train always stopped for a half-hour at meal times.

"If we eat quickly enough," Lottie told Miss Safford, "we can take a walk up and down the station platform."

"Good," Miss Safford agreed.

Other passengers were glad to get a little fresh air and exercise, too. Sometimes they would stop and chat with each other.

"So you are going all the way to 'Frisco," said one gentleman. "You have an exciting trip ahead of you."

"It has been exciting enough already," Lottie told him.

"But just wait until you start down the Sierra. There is a stretch there where the road drops five thousand feet in less than three hours. Either you will think it is wonderful or you'll be scared to death or maybe both. One thing is certain. You will take off your hat to the men who planned and built such a railroad."

He was right. Lottie gasped when the train started its exciting rush down the mountains. It whirled around curves. It plunged through dense forests. It ran along the edge of great chasms with rushing water far below. But she thought of more than the men who had made the road. She thought, too, of the Creator who had made the mountains. "And he made, too, the men who have conquered them." The eighth Psalm ran like music through her mind!

What is man that thou art mindful of him . . .? Thou madest him to have dominion over the works of thy hands . . . O Lord, how excellent is thy name in all the earth!

At last they were on level land once more. In California the tracks ran through rich farmland. There were houses with broad porches. But they didn't look like the ones in Virginia.

"I've left my home on the other side of the mountains," thought Lottie Moon. "I've left my old life there, too."

There was no time to be homesick. San Francisco was just ahead of them. San Francisco was the gateway to her new world.

She had only two days to spend in the new western city. They were busy days. Last arrangements must be made. Last letters must be sent home. She had time, though, to see a little of the city. She saw, too, her first Chinese not in a picture.

"There are over fifty thousand of them here in the city," she was told. "They were brought over, you know, to help build the railroad. Now they work in factories, in laundries—everywhere. They are good workers. You should see the wooden shanties they built for themselves, with their roofs made of flattened tin cans.

"And you should hear the noise they make when their New Year comes in. Why, last year, when it was all over, the city had to sweep up over a hundred bushels of exploded firecrackers in just one street!

"If you want to work with the Chinese, Miss Lottie, you can do it right here without leaving the United States."

Lottie shook her head. There was plenty of work to be done here. That was plain. But there were others who could do it. Her own work lay thousands of miles away, with the women and children of China. On September 1, 1873, her ship steamed out of San Francisco Bay.

"You should hear the noise they make."

11
Across the Pacific

"No one needs to worry about what to do during his first days aboard a ship," Lottie told Miss Safford. "The ocean takes care of that for you."

The ocean did. Almost before they lost sight of land Lottie was seasick. She didn't want supper that night. The next morning she cared even less for breakfast. But the weather was good and the sun was shining. Finally she dragged herself up on deck. There she felt better quickly.

Already the ship's passengers were beginning to

make friends with each other. More than one of them stopped at Lottie's chair.

"You will be well in less than no time, now," they said cheerily.

She was. By that very afternoon she, too, was walking up and down the deck. She was stopping to cheer the folks who hadn't become well as quickly as she had.

It was a jolly group of men and women aboard the big vessel. Soon they were playing games together. They played tricks on each other like naughty schoolboys. Miss Moon laughed at their jokes and their skylarking. It was fun to be with them.

Even more, though, she enjoyed the hours when she and Miss Safford sat in a quiet corner of the deck. They talked about their work and their plans. Miss Safford was to be a missionary under the Presbyterian church; Miss Moon under the Baptist. Their fields would be far apart. Would they ever see each other again after they docked?

"We can write to each other, anyway," said Lottie. "Maybe some day we can write to each other in Chinese."

One day while Miss Safford was busy in her cabin, Lottie sat alone. She looked out over the blue waters. Now it was not only the mountains that separated her from her old home. There was a broad strip of ocean, too, and it was growing broader every day.

"I remember when I left home to go to the Virginia Female Seminary," she thought. "How I longed to turn around and go back! But that isn't the way I feel now. Not at all."

A young girl walked past her several times. Her face looked cloudy and unhappy. Once she stopped by Lottie.

"May I sit here?" she asked suddenly, pointing to Miss Safford's empty chair.

"Certainly," Lottie smiled. She had taught young girls. She knew that sometimes it did them good to talk.

"I declare," the girl said. "I don't know which is worse—to be seasick or to be homesick."

"Both can be pretty bad."

"Aren't you homesick right now? I am."

Lottie shook her head. "Home is where the heart is," she quoted. "You've left your heart behind you, so, of course, you are homesick. I've sent mine on ahead. That is why I am anxious to get there."

Japan! The beauty of it! Its strangeness! Lottie's heart caught in her throat. It seemed as if she were walking in a dream. She went through the little shops, with their beautiful silks. She saw the small farms, which were tended so carefully that not a leaf seemed out of place. There were mulberry trees which reminded her of those in the yard at Viewmont. And the small men and women! They were so polite, so careful, so anxious!

"I could stay here for weeks!" she told Miss Safford.

But they had to hurry on. The last lap of their long journey was still ahead of them.

Lottie had just crossed the largest ocean in the world. No wonder that she felt as if the East China Sea were a very small body of water. She was sure it would take only a short time to cross over to Shanghai and then sail up along the coast to Chefoo. Many of her fellow passengers had told her good-by in Japan, but there were still some of her old friends aboard. There was a new friend, too—Mrs. Crawford. She and her husband had been missionaries a good many years. They had been taking a short rest. Now Mrs. Crawford and Miss Moon would make the last part of the trip together. Mr. Crawford would follow in a few days.

"It seems almost like coming home to be aboard ship once more," Lottie told Mrs. Crawford as they boarded the ship to cross the China Sea. "Only this is such a short trip we'll hardly have time to settle down."

Mrs. Crawford agreed. "I hope it will be a pleasant one, too."

"Of course it will. The weather is beautiful. And the sea is so smooth!"

"Maybe." Mrs. Crawford looked doubtful. She knew the sudden danger that could sweep over the China Sea.

Lottie was soon to know it, too. Suddenly the sun was gone. The wind was rising. Almost before she could realize what was happening it was lashing the sea into white-capped waves. They dashed against the ship. They washed across her decks. They battered against her sides. When the rain came, it beat down so heavily it seemed almost to flatten down the waves.

Could any ship ride out such a storm? Lottie wasn't at all sure. Was she to give her life for China before she had even lived there? How the wind howled! But there had been another storm once, on a sea far from here. And Christ had spoken to the waves, "Peace, be still." Would he

The storm lasted all night.

quiet the storm here as he had on Galilee? Perhaps. Perhaps not. Either way, he was with her. There was nothing of which she needed to be afraid.

The storm lasted all night. Then its end was as sudden as its beginning. The wind died away. The rain stopped. The sun came out.

Their ship had been so badly battered it had to go back to port for repairs. Soon, though, they were on their way again. And, at last, they reached Chefoo.

From Chefoo, it was only fifty-five miles to Tengchow. Tengchow was a walled city. It had been built at least a thousand years before. It was an important city. Students came to Tengchow to take examinations for work with the government.

It was at Tengchow, too, that Edmonia was waiting for her. Nearly three years had gone by since she had seen the young woman she still thought of as "little sister." Lottie wasn't even thinking about Edmonia, though, when she came at last to the walls of the city. She was thinking about the women and children in Tengchow. These were the people whom she had come halfway around the world to help. Here, inside the walled city, was her new home.

12
New Home

S<small>TUDY</small>! S<small>TUDY</small>! S<small>TUDY</small>! Lottie had been a good student at the Virginia Female Seminary. At the Albemarle Female Institute she had been even better. But in neither place had she ever studied as she did now. Morning, noon, and night! It was always the same subject—Chinese. Until she could speak and understand the language, this strange foreign city around her was just a big Chinese puzzle.

She watched the women who went by the mission. How could they even toddle on those tiny, bound feet? She watched the children with their round faces and their slanted black eyes.

"I love them already," she told Edmonia, "but there is so much for me to learn before I can help them."

Edmonia nodded. "I used to feel the same way myself. You don't see how you can ever understand folk who do everything backwards."

"Exactly. Of course, they probably think I do everything backwards, too, but goodness me! My teacher starts me at the back of my book instead of the front. I must read from right to left. If I want to shake hands with a friend, I must shake my own hands instead. Why, even when I say my lesson, it is only polite for me to stand with my back to the teacher!"

The sisters laughed together.

"And the Chinese say their last names first," Edmonia reminded her. "The men wear long skirts while the girls wear trousers."

"And they eat only two meals a day," Lottie

agreed. "Really, though, that is sensible. Think how much time the women save in their cooking and cleaning up. I like the way they dress, too. Those long, loose jackets must be downright comfortable. I don't believe they cost as much as American clothes, either. Some day I am going to try them—but not yet. The first thing I have to do is to work away on this language."

Work away she did. October turned into November. It wasn't very different from the Novembers back home. There were still a few leaves left on the trees. For several days, though, the wind had been chilly and biting.

"It will soon be two-suits cold," Edmonia told Lottie. "Very few people here have stoves, you know. When folks get cold, they just put on another suit of clothes. By the time it is three-suits cold, even the children who are almost starving look like little butterballs."

At last there came a clear sunny day. It was too pretty to stay indoors.

"We're going on a picnic," Mrs. Crawford called to Lottie. "You come along, too."

Lottie shook her head firmly. "I can't possibly spare a whole day from my books."

"You won't be wasting your time. That I promise you. I called it a picnic because we'll carry our own dinner and eat it outdoors. But we aren't just off for a holiday. We are going on a one-day preaching trip to the women in the villages outside the city."

"You've had enough of books for a while," Edmonia added. "It is time now to listen to the Chinese people talking and see how much you can understand."

That sounded sensible. Lottie put away her books. In less than no time she was ready to join the others.

Mrs. Holmes was the fourth woman at the mission. Her husband had been killed by bandits nearly fifteen years ago. Did that make her hate the Chinese? It did not. Instead, she had stayed on and on in their country. She had helped them in every way she could.

Now it was she who led the way down the narrow street. She was riding a donkey. It was a nice donkey. It never even tried to kick, but how it could bray!

"I am glad we're not trying to slip up on somebody without being heard," Lottie decided.

The three other women went in chairs. Each was carried on long poles by two men. "It is the easiest of all ways to travel," Edmonia told her. "Just wait until you have tried some of the others."

"A donkey cart, for instance," said Mrs. Crawford. "They never have any springs, you know, or any curtains in the back. You certainly get all the fresh air you want. And the last time I rode in one I didn't see the cobwebs under the top. My hair was covered with them when I got out."

Oh, what crowds! And what a noise! The shops all had open fronts. There were big piles of fruit and vegetables by the side of a little bridge.

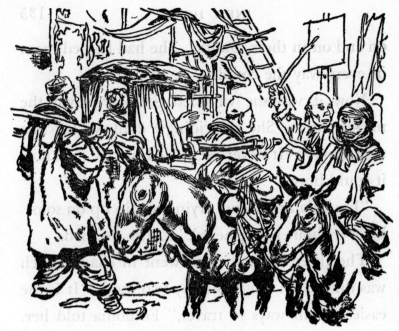

"Oh, what crowds!"

It seemed to Lottie as if each peddler were trying to outshout all the others.

Men carrying baskets on each end of a long pole pushed their way through the crowds. Even Lottie could tell their shouts meant "Open up! Open up!"

In the midst of all the noise she heard a bell. Just as she leaned forward to see what it was, her bearers jerked to one side. She almost went over

Each peddler was trying to out shout the others.

backwards. The men flattened themselves against the nearest wall. From all the shaking and tumbling, Lottie thought for a second her chair would be mashed flat with her inside. She finally managed to pull herself forward and peep through the curtains again. Why, it was only a man trying to make a way for his mules down the narrow road! At last they reached the city gates and went through them into the countryside. Lottie sank back. She felt as tired as if she, herself, and not her bearers, had been pushing her way through to the gate.

There were many small villages outside the city.

"The farmers," Edmonia told Lottie, "go out to the farm during the day, but they stay in the villages at night. They are safer from bandits that way."

In the first of the little villages the chair men set down their loads. Mrs. Holmes got down from her donkey.

Lottie looked around. Surely the Chinese women would be glad to see her. She had come so far to help them. They would come eagerly to listen to Mrs. Holmes and the others. She, herself, could learn new words listening to them.

But the women did not come. A few of them peeped out through the doors of their little houses. They made Lottie think of the squirrels in the trees back home, peeping through the branches. Like the squirrels, the women ran away quickly at the slightest move toward them.

Lottie was disappointed but the other missionaries didn't seem surprised, and at last they went on to another village. Here the women weren't quite so frightened. They stood at their house doors and looked as if they were ready to listen. But an old man came along. He spoke to them angrily and pointed with his hands. Lottie could tell he was ordering the women inside. He called the missionaries a word Lottie hadn't recognized. She was sure she had not heard it before. She asked Edmonia what it meant.

"Foreign devils," said Edmonia, her eyes twinkling.

"Oh! Well, that is one word I shan't try to learn."

Edmonia laughed. "You'll hear it so often you will learn it without trying. But I don't suppose you will ever get so you like it."

At last they reached a village where the story

of Christ had been told before. The women were no longer afraid. They gathered around and listened eagerly.

When Mrs. Holmes had finished her talk to them it was past time for the picnic dinner. The crowd had no intention of going away. They pressed closer than ever to watch Lottie open the dinner basket. She hardly had enough room to spread out her napkin. But she didn't mind; she was too busy listening to them.

Lottie was delighted to find that she could understand some of their eager questions. "What is that?" asked one woman, pointing at her fork. "What's that?" asked another, pointing at the biscuit in her hand.

Lottie tucked the words away in her mind. "Now I know how to say 'What's that?'"

Mrs. Crawford, by her side, translated some of the other questions. "What is that strange food you are eating?" "Why did your mother never bind your feet?" "Why do you have blue eyes?

Only devils have blue eyes." "Are you married?"
"How old are you?" The questions lasted through
the dinner.

Afterwards, Lottie repacked the basket while
the other women started their teaching again. As
she looked up she saw a group of children standing
under a tree close by, watching her. She went over
to them and, at first, they drew back. They were
half shy, half afraid. The smallest boy started to
run, but the biggest boy stood still until she was
close enough to touch the top he was carrying.

"What is that?" Lottie asked. She was trying
out her new words.

The little boy stopped running to listen. Slowly
he came back. "He probably feels that there is no
need to be afraid of a foreign devil who doesn't
even have sense enough to know what a top is,"
Lottie thought, amused.

The older boy was too shy to answer. He looked
at Lottie with his mouth open. It was the little
boy who spoke up bravely.

"It is a top," he told her, solemnly, his eyes big and round.

Lottie tried not to laugh at his shining eyes and his funny little pigtail. She said the word after him as solemnly as he had. Then she touched his jacket, his cap, even his hand. Soon they were making a game of it. The children were no longer solemn. They laughed when her tongue got twisted over the new sounds. When the other women were ready to start home Lottie thought she had never learned so much in such a short time.

"I must give my new friend a gift first," said Lottie to Edmonia.

She handed the little boy a small book with a red cover. It told the Jesus story in words that children could understand. The little boy didn't open the book, but he ran his fingers over the cover again and again. He liked the red cover very much indeed.

"Will you tell him," Lottie asked Mrs. Crawford, "that I want him to read what is inside. When I come again I shall talk to him about it."

The chair bearers had brought her chair. They set it down for her to step in. It was good to sit down again. Lottie hadn't realized how tired she was. How many new words she had learned today! "What is it?" "Top." "Hand." "Cap." She repeated them to herself to make sure she remembered them all.

After a while she peeped through her curtains. It was nearly sundown. On one side of the path lay the sea. Far off there were several islands. A lone sail caught the light of the setting sun. On the other side of the path the farmers were still in their fields, bending low over their work.

"It looks so beautiful, so peaceful," Lottie said to herself, "but it isn't, not really. These poor hard-working people have no hope of anything better."

13
Busy in the Country

LOTTIE'S CHAIR men grunted as they jogged along the narrow dirt road. The chill November wind whistled in through the cracks of her covered chair.

Lottie shivered. "This is what Father used to call 'raw weather' back at Viewmont," she said.

For a moment her mind was filled with memories of those old Viewmont days. "On an afternoon like this I used to curl up in a chair in front of the fireplace with a book and a juicy apple. Oh, me!"

How long ago that Viewmont life was! Why, she had been in China now for nearly ten years!

Ten years! Lottie smiled as she remembered her early struggles with the language, but the smile faded as she thought of the months when Edmonia had been so ill. They had tried so hard to make her well but, at last, there was nothing to do but to take her back to America. Lottie missed her little sister terribly. The smile came back as Lottie remembered how she, herself, had come back to her loved China. She thought of the girls' school she had started. There had been—and her face grew sober again—the famine. There had been—

The chair bearers were lowering their load to the ground. It was late afternoon. This would be the last village she and Mrs. Holmes could visit today.

The children crowded around her before she could get out of the chair. A big boy held up a little book. Its red cover was worn.

"You gave me this last time!" the boy told her proudly.

"And do you know the Jesus story it tells?"

Lottie began to ask questions. The boy answered happily. Why, it was years since she had been here. How well he remembered!

Mrs. Holmes was equally busy with the women to whom she was talking. Both of them hated to leave the village when the time came. So did the chair bearers. It would be a long trip back to town. While Mrs. Holmes and Miss Moon were busy the men had gone off quietly down the village street. Their faces were happy as they came back.

"We have found a place for you to spend the night," they told the two women.

Lottie and Mrs. Holmes were delighted, too. Very often no one in a village was willing to take in the "foreign devils." It would be good not to have to go back to town. Now they could get a much earlier start tomorrow to the next village.

The village women and children followed excitedly as they started down the narrow street. They crowded close when the missionaries reached the home the chair bearers had found for them.

The room they were to share together was bare but comfortable. At one end was the *kang*.

Lottie remembered how puzzled she was the first time she saw a *kang*. What in the world was it? She soon found that it was the most useful piece of furniture in the home. It was a brick platform across the end of the room, just about chair-high. In a space underneath a small fire was built. When the bricks got hot they stayed warm all night. During the day the *kang* could be used for a seat. When night came, the whole family could sleep on it. No wonder there was a *kang* in nearly every house. It was a stove, a chair, and a bed all in one. Sometimes it was the only piece of furniture in the room, but no more was needed.

As was usual in most houses, a mat was spread over the top of the *kang*, with a rug on top of the mat. Both rug and mat could be put under a person if the bricks were too hot. On a chilly night like this, though, Lottie decided as she sat down, the warm bricks were downright comfortable. She rolled up her quilt for a backrest and began to teach again.

"If only our work could always be as pleasant as this!" thought Lottie.

Of course it couldn't be. Sunset the next day found Lottie and Mrs. Holmes far from home.

The warm bricks were downright comfortable.

They had visited ten villages. They were worn out. Their bodies ached with tiredness. And they were hungry. Lottie's throat throbbed. It was still hard for her to speak Chinese, and the heavy words tired the muscles of her throat.

"I just can't talk any more today," she told Mrs. Holmes.

But when they reached the next village the women and children came crowding around their chairs once more. What could she do? Sore throat or not, she must tell them of Christ.

At last, worn out, they started off to the room which their chair bearers had found for them. Would it be as comfortable as last night's lodging?

Lottie knew she could hardly hope for that, but she hadn't thought it *could* be quite as bad as it was. The little room was hardly more than nine feet square. The rafters were almost low enough to touch. They and the walls were black with smoke. The matting on the mud *kang* was dusty.

There was only one window, high up. It was covered with paper and couldn't be opened. The only doorway had no door. It opened into another room where the chair bearers would sleep.

But what difference did all that make? The important thing was that the people were anxious to hear about Christ. The little room was soon crowded. Lottie forgot her aching throat. She forgot the stuffy, stifling room—the heat, the smells, the smoke. She talked on and on. When their guests were finally gone she and Mrs. Holmes hung a shawl over the doorway and went to sleep on the dusty old *kang*.

The next morning their visitors arrived before they had finished breakfast. Soon there were over thirty people in the little room. Some boys climbed on a table outside to get a better look at these strange foreign women. Others tore holes in the paper window to peep in.

Of course not all of the people were interested in hearing about God. Many were just curious.

Often they would interrupt Lottie to ask: "How old are you?"; "Why don't you wear earrings?"; "Did you make these shoes you have on?"; "Which country do you like best—yours or ours?"

Lottie was used to this. Sometimes she wished she had a talking machine to grind out the answers. Instead, she would reply politely and then go on with her teaching.

"We have never seen such heavenly people before," she heard one woman outside the door remark. That was certainly better than being called a "devil old woman." She and Mrs. Holmes were as happy as they were tired when at last they started back home.

"Am I too happy?" Lottie wondered. "No. That is not exactly what I mean. Do I let myself become happy too easily? Do these friendly people make me forget the thousands and hundreds of thousands who have never heard of Christ?

"Take Pingtu, for instance. How the people there hate foreigners! If we tried to visit them we'd be risking our lives every mile of the way. But suppose—"

There was little time in Lottie Moon's life to spend in supposing. Her everyday duties crowded too closely around her. To add to her burdens, the time came when Mrs. Holmes had to go back to America. Lottie took over her little house. Really, it was three small houses, with a big wall fastening them together. They were built around a little yard. The houses were over three hundred years old. They had no floors. The tiny windows were made of paper.

Lottie began to make this "House at the Little Cross Roads" into a comfortable home. They had wooden floors put down. They tore out the paper and put glass panes in the windows. Lottie planted a rosebush by the porch and a crepe myrtle bush in the yard.

It was a busy life that she led in the Little House. She had her schools, her church work in Tengchow, her work with the women and children in the villages outside the city. Still, she couldn't forget the women in Pingtu.

"Some day—" she promised herself. And Lottie Moon always kept her promises.

14

More Cookies

THE NIGHT was so dark that even the stars looked
dim and useless. A biting wind whipped under
the top of Lottie's *shentza*. She shivered, but it
wasn't only because of the cold. There was excitement in that shiver, too.

Suddenly the front mule stopped. The *shentza*
was a cart on two long poles instead of wheels.
One mule carried these shafts in front and another
in back of the cart. When the front mule stopped,
the back mule kept moving, and the *shentza* was
pushed forward so hard that Lottie nearly tumbled

on her face. That was bad enough, but worse still, the bells on the mules' harness jangled angrily. Lottie held her breath.

A dark shape appeared by the side of the *shentza,* Was it a bandit? Her heart was in her mouth. But the voice that came out of the darkness was Mr. Chao's. He was her guide on this dangerous trip.

"Give me some straw," he whispered. "We must muffle these harness bells. If anyone should hear us—"

He didn't finish the sentence. He didn't need to. Lottie knew.

The few things she had been able to bring with her were on the floor of the *shentza.* She had covered them first with straw and then with a blanket to sit on. Now she reached under the blanket and pulled out some straw for Mr. Chao. He stuffed it into the harness bells.

They started on again stealthily. The bells were quiet. But suppose one of the mules should bray the way Mrs. Holmes' donkey used to do! Or sup-

"Give me some straw," he said.

pose one of them balked and decided to lie down! The driver could never get him up without making a noise.

A noise would waken the people in the little houses by the roadside. That, Lottie knew, would be the end of her journey. The people of Laichowfu hated foreigners. Prison would be the best she could expect if she were caught in their city, perhaps death.

It wasn't the fault of these inland Chinese—not really. They had been told such terrible stories about "the foreign devils."

"They honestly believe we try to steal their children," Lottie reminded herself. "They think we cut out their hearts and their eyes. No wonder they hate us."

It had been hard to frighten Lottie Moon when she was a little girl. It was harder than ever now. Maybe her heart beat faster than usual as her mules jogged softly through the dark, sleeping city. She sat far back in the *shentza,* like a small child playing hide-and-seek in an overturned water barrel.

But the prayer she was praying was not for herself. It was for the people of Laichowfu. She prayed that their hatred might be turned to love of the true God. When daylight came Laichowfu was far behind her.

Mr. Chao had worked in Mrs. Crawford's home. He had become a Christian there. His people lived in Pingtu, and he was very anxious to have them hear the Jesus story, too. That was why he had left the Crawfords to show Miss Moon the way to his old home and to help her after she got there.

"You can stay in my mother's home at first," he told her. "Then I can help you get a house of your own."

He did. It was a small house. There was no American furniture. Lottie had to sleep on a *kang*. She was glad to do it for if she wanted the Chinese women to become her friends, she must live as they did. She began to wear Chinese clothes. She ate Chinese food. She tried every way to make friends.

But the women and children in the neighborhood were still afraid of her. They passed her house with timid steps. They stole quick, frightened looks at her when she spoke to them, but they would not come into her house.

"How can I show them," puzzled Lottie, "that I am really their friend? If only I could get the children to come, their mothers would soon follow."

What could she do? What would children like best? Toys? She hadn't been able to bring any with her. Food? Suddenly she smiled. She was remembering Little Girl Lottie making her first batch of cookies.

"I wonder if Chinese children would like them as much as I did."

Mr. Chao was her cook now. The next morning she asked him, "Do you suppose you could make some little American cakes if I told you how?"

"Can try," said Mr. Chao cheerfully.

Later that morning the delicious odor of baking cookies filled the courtyard of the little house.

Lottie, working at her desk, sniffed it delightedly. She felt as if she were back in Viewmont.

Three little boys who were passing the entrance sniffed, too. They were just such little boys as Lottie especially liked. Their little round faces with their heads shaved except for long pigtails, were turned for one more whiff of the strange delightful smell.

They moved out of sight but it wasn't long before they were back, peeping in at the gate entrance. They pushed each other into the doorway, then ran away. When they peeped through the gate again, they saw the "devil old woman" coming across the courtyard toward them. She was carrying a plate filled with little cakes. So that was where the fine smell came from!

"Won't you have one?" she held out the plate.

The little boys tumbled over each other backing away, but they didn't back very far. The cookies looked too good.

"She doesn't talk devil-talk," one of them whis-

The bravest boy came closer.

pered to the others. "She talks just like we do."

"Her clothes are like my mother's," said another.

"But look at her big feet!"

Lottie Moon was still smiling. She held out the plate of cookies a little farther. At last the bravest of the boys came closer—very, very slowly. Then he made a grab. He dashed back to the others with a warm cookie in his hand.

Rather fearfully he nibbled it. It tasted as fine

162   HER OWN WAY

as it smelled. He took a bigger bite, then a bigger.
The other boys watched him anxiously. Would he
drop down dead? Nothing happened.

"It was good," he told them.

"Have another," said Miss Moon.

He took a second cookie. Now the other boys
dared try one, too. When they left at last, the
cookies were gone, but the boys and Lottie had
become good friends. It wasn't long until, just
as she expected, their mothers became friendly,
too. Soon she was as busy as ever she had been in
Tengchow—and just as anxious, too.

"I am such a very small drop in such a big
ocean," she realized. "We ought to have many
more workers here. Why, there are only eight missionaries in this whole big province of Shangtung!
Eight! We need a hundred!"

She wrote back to America again and again,
"Send on the missionaries!"

"But we have no money to pay their salaries,"
the mission board wrote back.

How could this difficulty be met? Day after day she worried about this problem. In 1887 Lottie Moon had an idea. "Why can't the women in the South," she wrote back home, "take a week in December for special prayers and offerings? Families and friends are giving Christmas gifts to each other then. Isn't it an especially good time to give gifts to Christ, too?"

There was a new missionary organization and the women who belonged felt that Miss Moon's idea was a good one. It would be their first big undertaking. All the next year they worked, getting ready for their first Christmas offering.

All the next year Lottie worked, too. It was over ten years now since she had come back to China. She was very tired. "Come back home and rest," her friends wrote her. But how could she, until there was some one to take her place?

It wasn't long until the Chinese New Year, and Lottie's work for these few weeks was not so heavy. During the days before the New Year it was impolite to go calling. Everyone was too busy getting ready for the holiday to have time to entertain guests.

Lottie knew what was going on in the homes around her. First, in nearly every kitchen in the town they were taking down the kitchen god from the wall where he had hung over the stove all the year, watching the family. Now he must be sent off to heaven to report. It was easy to teach Chinese children "Thou, God, seest me." That was what the kitchen god did all the year around. But to show them how different God really was from the picture on the scrap of paper that looked like a comic valentine, that was harder work.

They were smearing the kitchen god's mouth with honey or molasses so that he would have to "talk sweet" about the family when he got to heaven. Next, very carefully, they held him over the fire until a tiny blue flame licked the edge of the paper. When it burst into a blaze, the god had gone to heaven! There would be no one to "tell" on the family until the New Year came in. At that time they would paste a new god up over the stove.

Finally, New Year's eve came. Lottie had never before heard anything like the noise, even in America. Firecrackers! Shouts! Barking dogs! No wonder that by morning everyone was worn out. The city became very quiet then. Everyone was either asleep or getting ready for a big dinner.

In the quiet of the New Year's morning Lottie sat at the door of her little house. As she looked out at the sleeping city, she was very happy. There had been a letter from home telling her about the Christmas offering. Of course, it was too soon to know how successful it would be. It would be weeks before all the reports could reach the home office, and it would take still longer for the news to reach her. But Lottie Moon was sure. When the women of the church worked together for God, only one thing could happen. There would be enough for one—maybe for two—new missionaries. This was a very happy New Year—for herself, but that wasn't important. With the new workers it would also be a happy New Year for China.

15
Busy in Town

"**I**t hurts!" the little girl in Lottie's lap wailed.

"I know it does, dear." Lottie carefully loosened the tight bandages on the small feet. "I'm sorry."

The little girl was so surprised she forgot her tears. "That's not the way Old Grandmother talks. She says 'Of course it hurts and the sooner a girl child learns to cry quietly, the better. Then she won't bother anyone.' "

"Pretty soon it is going to stop hurting. Then you won't cry at all," Lottie said as she lifted the child from her lap. "There! That is enough for today. Run along and play with the other children for a while."

"Old Grandmother never tells me to run and play. She says girl children must 'rise, run, work, eat little, be silent, keep out of sight, and obey.' " The child spoke as if she were reciting a lesson.

"That is a lot for one little girl to do. Now, run along."

Miss Moon watched the child join the other youngsters in the yard.

"Thank goodness her father let me start unbinding those poor little feet before the bones were crushed. I don't want any girls with bound feet in my schools."

It had been hard to get fathers to believe that at first. And women like Old Grandmother were indignant.

"Of course the child's feet must be bound," Old Grandmother had stormed. "What man would ever marry a girl with big feet?"

She had looked at Lottie's feet as she spoke. She

was too polite to say "You see, *you* never got married," but Lottie knew what she meant.

Lottie laughed now as she remembered the look on Old Grandmother's face. "All the same," she told herself, "the movement against binding girl children's feet is growing. And I am one of those who helped start it."

She turned to go across the yard to the rooms in the house at the Little Crossroads which were saved for her own use. At the street door she stopped. There stood a group of beggars.

"Pity! Have pity!" they called to her, but it was a low cry. They knew they didn't need to wail as they did in the streets. Loud wailing didn't do a bit of good with "Law Moo Guniang," the Reverend Miss Moon. She would help them all she could, anyway.

She went to her room for her string of cash. Her Chinese money was made of brass. Each coin had a hole in the middle and was hung with the other coins on a long string. The money string was heavy, but it could buy so little nowadays. Even the dried grass which poor people used to make their fires with cost ten cash for little more than a pound!

Li Si Fu, the cook, came to the door to talk about dinner. He watched anxiously while Miss Moon took some cash from the string. He shook his head.

"But how can I eat while they are hungry?" she asked.

"If Law Moo Guniang gives away all that she has, then she, too, will starve."

But he knew there was no use in arguing. Law Moo Guniang would rather help other folks than eat, anyway.

Lottie's face was still sad after the beggars had gone.

"It is better than last year," she told Li Si Fu. "There were more of them then, and I could hear their cries all day long. But it is still bad."

"Drought means poor harvest. Poor harvest means famine," Li Si Fu said.

"And people who are weak with hunger are quick to come down with fever or the plague."

"So it is," her cook agreed, "and so it has been for many years. Now, will Law Moo Guniang tell me what to fix for dinner?"

"How can I think about my own dinner? Just make it very, very simple."

"There are guests."

In her sorrow over the beggars Lottie had forgotten her guests. Certain rooms in her home were always set aside especially for her Chinese friends. A woman who had been one of Lottie's pupils years ago had come with her little boy for a visit.

"Oyster soup," Lottie decided. "They will like oyster soup." As Li Si Fu turned away she added, "After you have dinner started, if you will come in I'll give you your English lesson. We'll read some in your Bible, too."

When Cook had gone, Lottie's thoughts went back to the starving people. She had seen mothers trying to give away their children so they would

be fed, but no one would take them. She knew
old women were dying in the streets from hunger
and cold. There were—but she mustn't think on
these things. She started to write a letter.

The door opened. Without even a "by-your-
leave" in walked two Chinese boys. Lottie stopped
them.

"You didn't knock," she reminded them firmly.

The boys looked at each other and grinned.
What crazy ideas this foreign woman had! Why
should they knock?

In walked two Chinese boys.

"In my country," Lottie told them, "it is always polite to knock at the street door, when it is closed."

The boys went out. They knocked at the door.

"Come in!" called Lottie.

They came in, still grinning. Their mother had sent them with a message. But they were in no hurry to leave after they had given it to her. The foreign woman's room was so queer! They had thought up two excuses to come call on her yesterday, and they hadn't finished looking at everything yet. How funny the pictures on the wall were! Did people really live in houses like that? And the carpet! It covered the whole floor.

"I don't believe she would even let us spit on it!" one boy whispered to the other.

They wished Law Moo Guniang would have dinner while they were there. People said she had knives at each place and cut her meat right at the table. How uncivilized! Even foreigners ought to know that Cook should cut the meat into very small pieces before it was brought in.

Lottie went back to her letter writing. The boys stood behind her. They breathed down her neck as they looked over her shoulder.

"What is that?" one of them asked, pointing to her pen. It didn't seem possible those funny scratches she was making could mean anything. "Why don't you use a brush, the way everyone else does?"

"In my country people use pens to write with."

"Oh!"

At last the boys left. Lottie hoped that now she could finish her letter in peace. But, no! The butter and milk man came. Four thousand cash for the month's milk! How much it cost to have guests! But some of these women had come in from the country for baptism. They must be taught and examined first, to make sure they understood what baptism meant. Some had come to ask questions about this new religion. Some had come to take communion. They could not get back to their homes in the country in a single day. And wasn't Law Moo Guniang their friend? Of course they would stay with her.

Once more she went back to her letter. Once more there came a caller. This time it was a Chinese gentleman, a member of the church. He wanted to talk church business.

If only he would say what he wanted to say and then go! But Lottie knew he would think it was impolite to do business that way. First he must ask about her health. She must ask about his. He must ask about her school. She must ask about his sons and the rest of his family. It would be quite a while before they could talk business.

She reached for her knitting. At least, she could be making a sacque for some poor baby while they talked. And the good brother wouldn't see how impatient she really felt.

"I made the boys be polite my way. Now I must be polite their way," Lottie said to herself.

At last her visitor was gone. So was most of Lottie's morning. She put away her work. There was time for one short call, but that was a happy one. On her way home she met one of her missionary friends.

"Something especially nice must have happened to you. You look so pleased!"

"It has," said Lottie, "and I am. I've just been visiting. When the little boy of the house saw me coming he ran to his mother. He didn't call me 'the devil old woman.' He said, 'Here comes the Heavenly Book Visitor!' Isn't that a wonderful name?"

16
War Again

THE HEAVENLY Book Visitor! How Lottie
Moon loved that name! And how she loved her
work! But that didn't mean that life was no longer
hard. Nor did it mean that all of China was ready
to listen to the missionaries.

In 1899 strange stories began to be whispered
about in the city. People were telling each other
about men from the North who were crying
"Down with the foreigner!"

"Boxers, they call themselves," Lottie's friends
whispered to her. "People say the Empress is en-
couraging them."

Soon the cry was "Death to all foreigners!" By 1900 thousands of hate-maddened people were trying to kill every foreigner in China.

"You must leave," the United States Government told the American missionaries. A Government ship was sent to take them away to safety.

Lottie didn't want to leave China. "I am not afraid. I must stay to help my Chinese friends."

Soon, though, it became plain that staying wouldn't help her friends a bit. The Boxers were not only trying to kill all foreigners. There was another cry, now. "Death to all who believe in the Foreign Devil's God!" They were trying to kill every Chinese Christian. Even to be seen with Lottie put her friends' lives in danger.

She fled, sadly, to Japan. There she joined the work of the missionaries to the Japanese. Her heart, though, was always back in China. When at last the Boxers were put down and it was safe for her friends, Lottie returned to Tengchow.

There were sad stories her friends had to tell

her. "The Boxers burned every Christian church and home they could. They killed every missionary they could find. They killed thirty thousand Chinese Christians."

Not all of her friends were there to tell her these stories. "Do you remember Brother Sun Hwe Teh? He was killed because he had some foreign medicines in his bag when the Boxers caught him. Pastor Li and some of the other Christians in Pingtu were tied to horses' tails by their queues and dragged for miles. Pastor Li escaped but most of the others died. They killed Old Chiang while he was praying, 'Father, forgive them.'"

"But they didn't kill Christianity in China!" they added proudly.

"No!" Lottie was as thrilled as they were. "It was like trying to put out a fire by scattering the coals. It only starts a new fire wherever the coals fall."

Certainly the mission work had never grown as it did after the Boxer rebellion. There were new churches. There was even a Christian hospital. Once, long ago, Lottie had had to steal through Laichowfu at night to keep from being killed. Now she helped to start a mission there.

Ten years went by. The children of her first school-children were in her schools now. Soon there would be the grandchildren.

"Why," thought Lottie in surprise, "I am growing old."

She didn't have much time to think about that, though. She had five schools to look after and was starting another one. She spent three days a week out in the country villages, telling the Jesus story. There just wasn't any time left to worry about herself.

Then in the midst of her busy life a new cloud arose. Lottie hardly knew when she first heard of it. Students, soldiers—even bandits—were joining together in a big army. "Nationalists." "Imperialists." "Down with the Emperor!" These were the words she heard wherever she went. She knew very well what they meant. They meant war! Revolution! And revolution would unloose the War Dragon over the whole country again. It wasn't only the soldiers who would be killed. Women and children, also, would face hunger and suffering and death.

It seemed more than likely that the missionaries would, too. "Each side will say you are helping the other," Lottie's friends told her. "That will give each side an excuse to rob and kill you."

The danger grew as the fighting came closer and closer. At last the word came that the missionaries should leave their homes and go to the coast. There an American ship could pick them up if it became necessary.

Tengchow was on the coast. Lottie wouldn't have to move just yet. Hwanghsien was inland. The missionaries and the doctor at the hospital there must leave.

"It isn't right," Lottie mourned. She remembered the Confederate War days, back in Virginia.

All the women who lived near the hospitals then helped to take care of the wounded. But they had had someone to show them what to do and how to do it. There would be no one left to lead the women at Hwanghsien after the doctor and the missionaries were gone.

Finally word came that there was fighting close to Hwanghsien. Lottie could stand it no longer. What difference did it make that she was seventy years old? Or that she was supposed to stay close to the coast for her own safety? Her Chinese friends needed her.

Quietly she packed a few things together. She didn't tell anyone about her plans. They would be sure to object. She slipped away as if she were going to spend the afternoon in one of the nearby villages. Instead, she kept on, along the road to Hwanghsien.

There had been fighting close by. The wounded were being carried into the city. The Chinese doctor who had worked with the mission doctor was doing all he could. Every cot in the hospital was filled. The church women were anxious to help, but the doctor was too busy to show them how.

Suddenly a surprising rumor ran through the hospital grounds! "The Heavenly Book Visitor is here."

No one could believe it. The women, nurses, doctor rushed to the front of the hospital. There stood Law Moo Guniang, her bags and bundles piled at her feet. She had come to stay.

The women crowded around her laughing and calling. Every one talked at once. Even the wounded soldiers inside could hear them.

"Cackle! Cackle!" grumbled one of the soldiers. "What a fuss women make!"

But Lottie hadn't come all the way from Tengchow just to talk. In less than no time she had taken off her hat and cloak. Her bundles were stored away in the doctor's own office.

"Now," she said briskly, "let's get to work."

When Lottie said work she meant work. It wasn't long before the hospital looked like another place. It was still overcrowded, but the cots were neat. The rooms were clean. There were fresh bandages for the Chinese doctor to use. Medicines were ready when he needed them.

Back at the coast the American missionary doctor was as restless as Lottie had been. At last there was a lull in the fighting. He made up his mind to go back to Hwanghsien.

"It isn't safe," his friends insisted.

"I'll just have to run the risk."

He got to Hwanghsien safely but with no time to spare. The two armies were closing together again.

Would the hospital still be there? Would it be burned? Or in ruins? He came down the narrow road almost sick with dread.

The hospital was there. It was running smoothly. And there was Lottie Moon, quietly showing her volunteer nurses how to cut and roll bandages.

There was still another surprise in store for the good doctor. When Lottie showed him around, she explained where things were. She told him what she had done. Then she added, "Now that you are here, I won't be needed any longer. I'll go back home this afternoon."

"Indeed you won't. The fighting has begun again along the Tengchow road. I just got through myself. You can never make it now."

Lottie smiled. "We'll see," she said.

She called one of the revolutionists who was

Not a gun was fired.

bringing in the wounded. He was a young man. Not many years ago he had been one of her school boys.

"Tell your general," she said, "that Miss Moon wants to pass through the lines on the Tengchow road this afternoon."

Then she called a man from the emperor's army and gave him the same message.

"Now," she said calmly, "I'll take a last look

She was going home.

around to make sure I am leaving everything straight. Then I can go."

It didn't seem at all unusual to her that a lone woman should ask two armies to stop fighting long enough for her to pass between their lines. She was their friend, wasn't she? Why, there were men in both armies who had known her for nearly forty years. She was helping their wounded, wasn't she? Of course they would let her through.

They did. Not a gun was fired as Lottie Moon passed calmly along the Tengchow road that afternoon. She had finished her work. She was going home to her House at the Little Cross Roads. Once again Lottie Moon had had her own way.

How Did It End?

LOTTIE MOON died in Japan in 1912. She was on
her way to America after a severe illness. Japanese
law required that her body be cremated, but lov-
ing friends brought her ashes back to America.
They are buried in the little cemetery at Crewe,
Virginia.

But that was not the end of her story. There is
no end to the story of Lottie Moon because her
work goes on. To Lottie, that would have been all
that mattered. That was her only reason for living.

So long as the spirit of missions stays alive, so

long as the work in which she believed so earnestly continues—in China or in any part of the world—so long will the story of Lottie Moon continue, too. It is the story of a woman who always had her own way because she made her way one with the way of Christ.